WASHOE COUNTY LIBRARY

3 123

D0397193

A New Owner's
Guide to
MINIATURE
SCHNAUZERS

JG-147

Overleaf: A Miniature Schnauzer adult and puppy photographed by Isabelle Francais.

Opposite page: Miniature Schnauzer Captain Sparkles McCoy, CD, TD, owned by Diane Gardner.

The Publisher wishes to thank the following owners of the dogs in this book: Sue Baines, Lynn Baitinger, Donna Marie Darling, June DiCiocco, Marge Ditz, Patricia Estes, Diane Gardner, Jane Gilbert, Mary Grundy, Ana Harris, Chris Kemper, Ollie Kerr, Gloria Lewis, Kristy D. Lockard, Mark Meeker, Tony and Dot Robbins, Charlotte Schwartz, Beatrice Smith, Norma Steill, Henrietta Tare, Janet Taylor, Linda Warner, Ruth Wise.

Photographers: Paulette Braun, BW Studios, Suzanne Crits, Nancy Fouts, Isabelle Francais, Tony and Dot Robbins, Charlotte Schwartz, Vince Serbin, Beatrice Smith, Robert Smith, Norma Steill, Karen Taylor.

The author acknowledges the contribution of Judy Iby for the following chapters: Sport of Purebred Dogs, Health Care, Identification and Finding the Lost Dog, Traveling with Your Dog, and Behavior and Canine Communication.

The portrayal of canine pet products in this book is for general instructive value only; the appearance of such products does not necessarily constitute an endorsement by the authors, the publisher, or the owners of the dogs portrayed in this book.

T.F.H. Publications, Inc.
One TFH Plaza
Third and Union Avenues
Neptune City, NJ 07753

Copyright © 2002 by T.F.H. Publications, Inc.

All rights reserved. No part of this publication may be reproduced, stored, or transmitted in any form, or by any means electronic, mechanical or otherwise, without written permission from T.F.H. Publications, except where permitted by law. Requests for permission or further information should be directed to the above address.

This book has been published with the intent to provide accurate and authoritative information in regard to the subject matter within. While every precaution has been taken in preparation of this book, the publisher and author assume no responsibility for errors or omissions. Neither is any liability assumed for damages resulting from the use of the information herein.

ISBN 0-7938-2796-5

If you purchased this book without a cover you should be aware that this book is stolen. It was reported as unsold and destroyed to the publisher and neither the author nor the publisher has received any payment for this "stripped book."

www.tfh.com

A NEW OWNER'S
GUIDE TO
MINIATURE
SCHNAUZERS

CHARLOTTE SCHWARTZ

Contents

2002 Edition

The Mini Schnauzer is a versatile and athletic dog.

Cattle drover, guard dog, cart puller—the Mini Schnauzer can do it all!

The Mini Schnauzer makes a wonderful addition to any family.

With patience and praise, your Mini Schnauzer will learn any command you wish to teach him.

The amiable and outgoing Mini Schnauzer can make friends with anyone!

INTRODUCTION to the Miniature Schnauzer

L
ike little men in gray tuxedos and sporting silver beards, Miniature Schnauzers are stylish little dogs that never fail to turn heads whenever and wherever they appear. They're also debonair and bright, with an opinion about almost everything they see, hear, and feel. Miniature Schnauzers do not sit quietly and watch life go on around them. They want to be a part of life and get in on all the action whenever possible. Because of their genetic heritage and innate intelligence, they are the quintessential partners in their owner's lives. And, I might add, I have known more than one Miniature Schnauzer who has literally altered the lifestyle of their owners because of this trait!

However they develop, they never lose their sense of humor or their love of life and all it has to offer. Even the oldsters are alert, curious, and eager to get involved. These qualities have endeared these dogs to Miniature Schnauzer lovers for 500 years, and will no doubt ensure them continued popularity in the canine kingdom for hundreds of years to come. So, dear reader, turn this page and let me introduce you to Miniature Schnauzers.

Full of humor and personality, the Miniature Schnauzer makes a wonderful pet.

Ch. Dargo's Rainbo Jam-Bo-Ree, owned by June DiCiocco, shows the distinctive look and expression that is part of the charm of the Miniature Schnauzer.

HISTORY of the Miniature Schnauzer

Welcome to the world of Miniature Schnauzers. This robust little terrier is every bit as intelligent and devoted to his master and family as he is strong and vigorous. He's also an amiable friend to those who show him kindness and friendship, yet a cause of deep concern to those who would threaten or harm him or his home and family. He is, after all, a Schnauzer—bright, curious, highly intelligent, fearless, and eager to please. His diminutive size makes him a miniature, yet his character and personality demand that he be recognized as an active participant in the world around him.

His traits can be attributed to his interesting origin. Many years ago, back in the 15th century, a Schnauzer of medium build was a valuable asset on German farms. He served as a drover of cattle, guard dog, and carting dog that pulled produce to market and guarded it while the farmer tended to the business of selling his products. The dog was also excellent ratter and worked tirelessly at keeping the rat population on the farm at a reasonable level.

Back in 1492, painter Albrecht Durer portrayed his own Schnauzer in a watercolor painting titled *Madonna with the Many*

Originally bred as a working dog, the Schnauzer proved to be a valuable asset to the farmers of Germany.

Cattle drover, guard dog, cart puller—the diligent Schnauzer's power and work ethic is famous.

Animals. In 1501, a famous tapestry was created depicting a Schnauzer. Then, in the 1600s, Rembrandt included a Schnauzer in one of his paintings.

From the medium-sized Schnauzer, a giant variety was developed. These powerful dogs served as police and guardians and continue that tradition in Europe and America today.

But it wasn't until the 1880s that serious breeding of Miniature Schnauzers in Germany commenced. There breeders reasoned that with the Schnauzer's history of being a working dog, they could keep the willingness to please, intelligence, and a love of family, and add a rough coat for protection to create the perfect German farm dog. Knowing how effective terriers in Great Britain were as family and farm dogs, they wanted to take the best characteristics of several breeds and create what would ultimately become the German farm and family dog.

By the late 1880s, smaller-sized Standard Schnauzers had bred with Affenpinschers to develop the smaller version of the breed. At the turn of the century, a male named "Peter von Westerberg" was a popular show dog and major contributing sire to the Miniature Schnauzer breed. Two other sires, "Prince von Rheinstein," born in 1903, and "Seiger Lord," born in 1904, were influential progenitors.

During these formative years, some wolfgrey Spitz, Poodle, and Brussels Griffon blood may have been used to set the genes for the salt and pepper or solid black coat and ratting instincts they carry today. Surely the Poodle would have contributed intelligence and a love of family, while the Affenpinscher would have given it a wiry coat.

Once the desired traits and characteristics were achieved, inbreeding (mating close relatives to each other) set the genes permanently. Thus, the Miniature Schnauzer was "fixed" for all time. As the breed was being developed in Germany, World War I began. This put a halt to nonessential activities, so the Miniature Schnauzer's development was placed on temporary hold.

With the end of World War I came a renewed interest in the breed, and in 1923, the first Miniature Schnauzer was imported to America. By 1925, the first Miniature Schnauzer litter was born on US soil, thus beginning the emergence of a most popular breed of dog.

The first American litter was produced by Mrs. Marie Slattery of the Marienhof kennels. That prefix, together with other equally well-known names such as Andrel, Handful, Geelong, Ledahof, Anfiger, Jonaire, and Allenhaus, became the backbone of the breed in America.

People began exhibiting Miniature Schnauzers at dog shows in Germany as early as 1899. In 1925, the first Miniature Schnauzers to be shown in America were a female named Amsel v.d. Criaksburg and her two daughters, Lotte and Lady. Chances are highly likely that American-born Miniature Schnauzers of today can trace their lineage back to Amsel and one of those early kennel prefixes.

Miniature Schnauzers were introduced in England in 1928. The breed has grown in popularity there ever since its debut. The most obvious difference between American Miniature Schnauzers and those of England and Europe is that only in America are breeders permitted to crop the ears, so the ears stand erect rather than fold over.

Originally, Miniature Schnauzers in America were exhibited along with Standard Schnauzers. This, however, presented a problem. The Standard is primarily a working dog and the Miniature, a terrier. Finally, in 1933, the distinction between the two Schnauzers was defined.

Crosses with other breeds, such as the Affenpincher, have contributed to the appearance and temperament of today's Mini Schnauzer.

The American Kennel Club officially accepted the American Miniature Schnauzer Club as the national regulatory organization for the breed. (National breed clubs set the Standard of Perfection for each breed and the American Kennel Club enforces those standards.) Thereafter, Standard Schnauzers were placed in the Working Group and Miniature Schnauzers in the Terrier Group.

As you'll discover throughout this book, there is a lot more to the Miniature Schnauzer than this history indicates. Not only are they a dog of antiquity, they are definitely a dog of the modern age. As dedicated as they were to their homes and families in the early days, they are just as staunch in their dedication to home and human companions today. Though their lifestyles have changed dramatically, they remain a robust friendly breed of dog that maintains a strong desire to function as part of the human pack. That, perhaps, is the secret to the charm of the Miniature Schnauzer.

CHARACTERISTICS of the Miniature Schnauzer

Miniature Schnauzers are handsome little terriers, squarely built with good muscle, possessing an abundance of energy and innate curiosity. They are friendly, often vocal, and devoted to those they consider pack members. From his larger cousin, the Miniature Schnauzer has inherited a repetoire of diverse behaviors, such as helping his owner with chores, fetching, carrying, and guarding. The dog's genes have helped him develop into the multitalented miniature version of the all-purpose Standard Schnauzer. Thus he is genetically programmed to be a highly intelligent companion.

In other words, the Miniature Schnauzer is more than a one-job dog. As one Mini owner said, "Whatever the Standard Schnauzer is, the Mini is even more so!"

Shyness, disobedience, and excessive aggression are unacceptable traits in the Miniature Schnauzer. He is not passive, but a spirited, alert, bright dog eager to please and be a fully functioning member of his family.

Visually, the Miniature Schnauzer is supposed to be a square dog with the same measurements from the top of his withers (shoulders)

A handsome squarely built terrier, the Miniature Schnauzer is a multitalented and intelligent companion.

The Miniature Schnauzer is a versatile and athletic dog that can be trained to do almost anything.

to the ground as from the stern (rump) to the chest. He must have a long flat skull, and his muzzle should be the same length from the tip of his nose to the stop (point between the eyes) as from the stop to the top of his skull (occipital bone).

The muzzle must be in proportion to the skull and, together with the topskull, must present a long rectangular appearance. Ears should be either cropped with pointed tips or V-shaped and carried bent over and close to the head. Teeth must be in a scissor bite, while his eyes must be deep set, oval, dark brown, and full of expression.

His neck should be strong and well arched, while the body must be short and deep with a topline parallel to the ground. His forelegs must be straight and, when groomed properly, the Miniature Schnauzer should appear to be standing on two straight posts. His hindquarters are well muscled and bent at the stifles as to allow the hocks to be perpendicular to the ground. The cropped tail, which is carried upright, should extend beyond the hocks.

The Miniature Schnauzer's unique double coat comes in three colors: solid black, black and silver, and salt and pepper.

In short, a Miniature Schnauzer is a picture of rectangles and square corners. He is never to appear rounded and sloping. When viewed from the side, even his underbody is flat and does not present a tucked-up look, seen in such breeds as Dalmatians and Whippets.

Just as his personality must be straightforward, so his body image must be clear, concise, and direct, with no hint of softness. He's a hardy little terrier, the epitome of the expression, "What you see is what you get."

Before attempting to decide whether or not you are the right person to own a Miniature Schnauzer, there are many things to consider. Not the least of these is a dedication to grooming. Unlike many short-coated breeds, Miniature Schnauzers require no small amount of attention to maintain good coat and appearance.

The ideal Miniature Schnauzers owner is one who has the time and the means to have the dog professionally groomed on a regular basis and to maintain the coat in between groomings. An alternative to this is the person who is willing and able to groom his own dog.

THE MINIATURE SCHNAUZER'S COAT

The Miniature Schnauzer actually has two coats, one a soft wooly undercoat and the other a stiff wiry outercoat. In addition there are three distinct colors permitted in the breed: solid black, black and silver, and salt and pepper. The most popular is probably the salt and pepper color.

Salt and pepper Miniature Schnauzers have light grey to silver undercoats. The wiry outercoat is made up of individually banded black and white hairs. In other words, if you were to examine a single outercoat hair of a salt and pepper dog, you would see that each hair is banded horizontally, with sections of black that alternate to white. This banding is what creates the salt and pepper look. How each hair is banded and how frequently the banding is repeated produces the degree of darkness in the salt and pepper coat.

Black and silver Miniature Schnauzers have solid black outer and undercoats on the head, neck, and body. Beards, eyebrows, and leg hairs are silver or white.

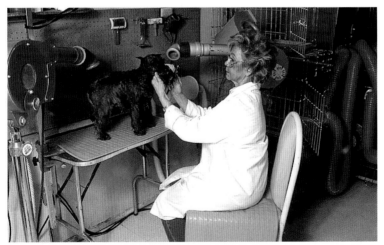

Regular grooming is necessary to keep the Miniature Schnauzer's coat in good condition and to keep the breed's signature terrier appearance.

In solid black Miniature Schnauzers, both the undercoat and the outercoat are to be true black, with no hint of tan or brown. Only in solid blacks is a small white chest patch permitted.

The distinctive beard and leg hairs of all Schnauzers are called furnishings. In the solid blacks, all furnishings must be black. In the salt and peppers, furnishings must be grey or pewter in color.

The pattern of wire and soft coat of the Miniature Schnauzer creates the distinguished elegance for which the breed is known. In all colors, the wiry outercoat appears on the head, neck, and body, while the whiskers, eyebrows, cheeks, throat, tail, and underbody are covered with the softer undercoat hairs.

A cursory glance at a Miniature Schnauzer shows a wiry-coated grey or black body with light grey or silver (except in the case of the solid blacks) furnishings. When you realize that Miniature Schnauzers are supposed to be rugged little dogs capable of performing tough jobs in all types of weather, the reason for the harsh wiry outercoat becomes apparent.

In terms of grooming, the Mini Schnauzer is a high-maintenance dog. The amount of time you want to spend on grooming should be a consideration when choosing a breed.

So far this description of the Miniature Schnauzer coat has referred to those dogs whose coats are maintained according to the requirements for exhibiting the dogs in the show ring. To achieve the combination of wiry and soft coat, the dogs must be plucked or stripped by hand. This entails pulling out the long hairs of the sections where the wire coat is desired.

Good grooming practices will not only keep your Miniature Schnauzer looking great, it will also keep his skin and coat healthy.

The process is called stripping and takes many weeks in order to get the wiry coat to come in at a rate that creates the most appealing look. Stripping is a job for professionals who specialize in show grooming. It takes many grooming sessions over several months, costs a considerable amount of money, and requires almost constant adjusting to achieve that perfect show coat.

Miniature Schnauzers do not shed. Their hair is similar to human hair in that it doesn't fall out—it just keeps growing. Thus they must be groomed on a regular basis in order to keep hair and skin healthy.

However, it is possible to own a Miniature Schnauzer and have it well groomed at all times without the major undertaking of professional show grooming. The alternative method is called clipping and utilizes electric sheers to create the lines and style typical of the breed.

The constant clipping of the wire coat will eventually change the hair to a soft grey or silver coat. This replacement of the harsh wire coat, however, does not change the overall appearance except to lighten the body color. It does allow the dog to be well groomed at all times and maintain that famous terrier look.

Many owners choose to have a professional groomer give the dog his haircut approximately every eight weeks while they maintain the coat in between grooming sessions. Others choose to groom their dogs themselves. Some people even take lessons in Schnauzer grooming before they embark on the process.

Later in this book we will discuss in detail the various aspects of keeping the Miniature Schnauzer looking good at all times, whether for a show career or life as a beloved companion. One thing is for sure, a Miniature Schnauzer must be groomed regularly all his life so, when considering one as a pet, the matter of grooming is a paramount consideration.

PERSONALITY

Now let's turn our attention to the Miniature Schnauzer's potential. After all, before taking a Miniature Schnauzer into your life, it is wise to know exactly what he is and is not capable of in terms of function and physical ability. Ideally, a breed's mental and physical abilities must match those of the people he lives with.

Do Miniature Schnauzers make good couch potato-type dogs? The answer is yes and no. They love to cuddle on the sofa with you, will lay in your lap for hours, will sleep on your bed while you rest or read, and will curl up beside you in front of the fireplace on a cold winter night.

However, they do not do well as exclusive couch potatoes. They're far too curious, alert, and active to be satisfied with a sedentary lifestyle. They need to get out and do things, go places with you, and play with their favorite toys at home.

Perhaps the best way to describe the Miniature Schnauzer is to say they are capable of all manner of physical activity, yet are equally content to alternate that busyness with moments of intimate calm shared with loved ones.

Miniature Schnauzers are good travelers and love riding in cars. A doggie safety belt is always recommended, and they quickly become accustomed to it if you train them to wear one right from puppyhood.

Visiting family and friends is a particular joy to them, and they usually receive more than their share of attention from hosts and guests alike. A well-trained Miniature Schnauzer is always a joy to live with and a wonder to those who see how obedient and mannerly he can be.

The ideal Miniature Schnauzer owner is one who combines times of physical activity with quiet times at home. In a word, Miniature Schnauzers are very versatile dogs.

When we speak of physical activities, what exactly are we talking about? Well, taking a swim in the family pool, going for a mile walk, jogging around the block in the crisp morning air, playing fetch on the front lawn, playing with gentle waves along the seashore, exploring the sights, sounds, and smells of the forest trail—these are all Miniature Schnauzer favorites and every one of them is good for humans, too! Suffice it to say that, pound for pound, a healthy Miniature Schnauzer makes a wonderful companion for those who appreciate a dog that wants and needs to be your partner in life.

Because of their intelligence, Miniature Schnauzers love learning. They can be taught a myriad of tricks and will perform them willingly for the acclaim they receive in exchange. Because they are strong and agile, they master running and jumping tricks quickly and excel at fetching and carrying. Bringing in the mail, carrying small parcels from one place to another in the home, and putting their own toys away at the end of the day are all activities they learn with ease.

Several Miniature Schnauzers I know fetch their own leashes when they want to go out to relieve themselves. Because they're so smart, they quickly associate their collars and leads with going for a walk. If the leashes are stored at a low level where the dogs can

The Miniature Schnauzer's love of activity and exercise will allow him to accompany you anywhere.

easily reach them, they almost teach themselves to carry the leashes to their owners—which translates into, "It's time to go out!"

Perhaps the one thing that Miniature Schnauzers are most famous for is their talent as alarm dogs. Their hearing is so much better than ours that they hear sounds we never hear—a car door slamming shut, a person walking along a footpath, car keys rattling outdoors, a person coughing. So when a stranger is nearby or a person is ringing your doorbell, the Miniature Schnauzer will not rest until you recognize that presence and assure the dog that all is well. In the case of unwanted intruders, the Miniature Schnauzer with his loud strong bark will cause the person to retreat in haste.

At one point in my career as a breeder and exhibitor of Miniature Schnauzers, I had 17 of them living in my big old farmhouse. They had their own room, each dog with his or her own crate, and each dog was free to run through the house, providing they were housebroken. When a visitor would come, it would take me several minutes to quiet them down and allow the guest to enter. Once quiet, however, they were perfect ladies and gentlemen and eagerly demonstrated their pleasure at seeing our guest without overwhelming the person.

A person with any degree of hearing loss could not choose a better companion than a Miniature Schnauzer. The dog will make certain that the owner never misses a sound in or out of the home. And if the owner doesn't investigate the source of the sound to the dog's satisfaction, the dog will run back and forth between the sound and the owner until the owner acknowledges the noise.

How do Miniature Schnauzers react to children and older people? Very well, providing the owner takes time to acclimate the dog to the various individuals who will be a part of the dog's life. As an example, during my Miniature Schnauzer days, I raised my grandson, Brett, at the same time the 17 dogs lived with us.

I made sure that every dog understood that Brett was to be respected and that they were to be kind and gentle. They also understood that they were never to bite or chew on his little arms or hands as he reached out to touch them.

Often times, I'd find Brett playing in one of the dogs' crates with his toys while the crate resident sat just beyond the entrance waiting patiently for the child to leave. Never once did a dog threaten Brett or cause him to be fearful. Thus the dogs and the child grew up loving and respecting each other.

In summary, Miniature Schnauzers do well with children, providing they are accustomed to them from puppyhood. When the dogs are introduced to children as adults, it may take some time and work on the owner's part to acclimate the dog, but with firmness and patience, it can be done.

Make sure the dog feels just as important and loved after the child arrives as he did before the child came into his life. I would not, however, force an older Miniature Schnauzer to accept a child if the dog obviously did not want to be near the child. In that case, I'd make sure the dog and the child were safely separated from each other and offer quality time and attention to both.

Regarding elderly people, Miniature Schnauzers seem to have a certain sense that tells them these folks are special. They are usually gentle, patient, and eager to sit quietly with the person for moments of peaceful togetherness. Somehow the dogs know that elderly people are for loving and children are for fun and activities.

As you can see, Miniature Schnauzers are extremely versatile and adaptable dogs. They tend to take life as they find it and adjust to new activities and situations easily without excessive moodiness, provided they are given fair treatment and understanding from the owner.

Sociable and affectionate, the Miniature Schnauzer is happiest in the company of people.

As I said before, they may be little in stature, but Miniature Schnauzers are huge in the things that go into making up the bigness of true canine companionship.

MINIATURE SCHNAUZERS TODAY

So often when we hear or read stories about dogs doing unusual things or helping people in unique ways, we learn that the dogs in question are large dogs. After all, German Shepherds, Rottweilers, Doberman Pinschers, and Komondors have been serving mankind for centuries. Many recognize the work done by Standard and Giant Schnauzers as drovers, guards, and cattle dogs. But how about small dogs?

Do they ever contribute to the well-being of mankind? Do they perform tasks that make life a little easier, a little more pleasant, and a little more rewarding for their human companions? Though they were developed as ratters and farm dogs, Miniature Schnauzers have accepted the challenge of the modern age and adjusted to present day lifestyles to be equally as productive and successful as companions and contributors in today's world.

I'll introduce you to some very accomplished Miniature Schnauzers who have really made a difference in the lives of the people they touched. And in doing so, I think you'll be duly impressed with this little dog.

First, meet Heidi. She lives with a lovely family consisting of mother, father, and two teenage boys. Becky, the mother, had a problem. Every afternoon she'd begin preparing dinner while her boys were upstairs in their bedroom playing the latest popular music. Trouble was they played the music loud enough to make the pictures on the wall rattle!

Well, when Becky was ready to serve dinner, she'd have to stop working in the kitchen and go upstairs to fetch the boys, because no amount of calling could break the sound barrier of their music. Her voice just wasn't loud enough. What to do? She needed to find a way to get the boys' attention without leaving the kitchen and fetching them in person.

About the same time that Becky was experiencing the desperation so typical of the parents of teenagers, Becky and Heidi were enrolled in an advanced obedience class. One of the assignments at that level of training included teaching the dogs to do a chore each day to help make the owner's life a little easier.

The Miniature Schnauzer's adaptable nature is sure to take him far! This "world-traveler" checks out the waves in Bermuda.

Enter Becky's creative imagination: Wouldn't it be great if Heidi could go fetch the boys instead of taking Becky away from the dinner preparations?

With a little help from her husband and full cooperation from the boys, Becky found a way. Heidi, once trained, would be in charge of rounding up the family for dinner every evening. And all it took was about ten days of practice and Heidi had the job down as if she were a pro at family fetching!

First, Becky's husband removed the latch and lock mechanism from the door of the boys' room. That way, they could shut the door to keep the sound down, yet the door could be easily pushed open by Heidi with a simple nudge of her nose.

Next, Becky gave the boys some dog biscuits and showed them how to encourage Heidi to push the door open, jump up on the bed, and bark for a biscuit. (This would translate later to "Come to dinner, boys! Mom has dinner ready and she's waiting!" Actually, this could also be used for calling the boys for purposes other than dinner and Heidi would still do her job as long as she knew she'd be rewarded for getting the boys' attention.)

This whole sequence of events began with Heidi and Becky in the kitchen. Becky would turn to Heidi and say, "Go get the boys!" at which time the boys would begin excitedly calling Heidi. They'd also say things like "Come get your cookies!" and "Here's a biscuit, Heidi!" to encourage her to race up to the top of the stairs where the boys waited with cookies and lots of praise.

Once Heidi caught on to running to the boys when Becky commanded "Go get the boys!" the teenagers began moving back toward their room, step by step, so that Heidi had to go further to reach the reward. Finally the boys were calling from their room and Heidi was still racing to them.

The final step was having the boys wean off calling Heidi and having her race to them with just Becky's command to fetch them. Two days of practicing this and Heidi understood exactly what she was supposed to do. The job's pattern of behavior was formed.

Incidentally, Heidi has been doing this chore for several years now and shows great enthusiasm for the work. It makes her feel important, needed, and very much appreciated. In short, it gives her a reason for being that demonstrates the self confidence typical of a well-bred Miniature Schnauzer.

Summoning teenagers to the dinner table is not the only chore Miniature Schnauzers can perform. I know of many that do all types of jobs to help their owners. Bringing in the newspaper every day is just one of them. I have several Miniature Schnauzer students who pick up their own toys at the end of each day and deposit them back in the basket where they belong. One even carries a can of beer placed in a little cloth bag by the wife in the kitchen to the husband out in the garden! Talk about handy!

Happiest when serving man, few Miniature Schnauzers forget their roots as a working dog.

"Want to go out?" asks one owner I know. The dog responds by fetching his collar and lead and bringing them to the owner. If the dog merely walks away and ignores the owner's question, that means, "No, I don't want to go out just now."

Several others eat their meals from

The playful and curious Mini Schnauzer will try anything once. Now all he needs to do is figure out how to get down!

stainless steel bowls and, when finished, bring the empty bowls to the owners for washing. I also know of several parents who wish they could train their children to help like that!

Carrying the car keys from the house to the car is an important job that Angus, a black and silver male student, does almost daily. He gets so excited when his owner gives him the keys because he knows that he's going for a ride. Miniature Schnauzers love riding in cars and Angus is no exception!

I took my own Angel's love of performance a step further than household chores when I taught her to track. Little did I know then that we were opening a door into a fascinating and challenging new world of olfactory work where Angel would be the leader and I, the follower. Let me tell you about it.

Angel was one of four puppies in a litter I bred. Both her mother and father were champions and very correct in conformation. They were also bright, intelligent, curious, and friendly. When Angel was six months old, I turned her over to a well-known Miniature Schnauzer breeder and professional dog show handler, Joan Huber of Blythewood Kennels.

From that moment on, Angel's life was a series of grooming sessions, show training lessons, and weekends on the road competing at dog shows. Initially I was pleased that she was a good enough specimen of her breed to become a champion. However, something kept nagging at me about her being away and not working with me in other activities.

When she was nine months old, I made the fateful decision. I'd take her off the show circuit and bring her home. Then she and I would begin tracking training.

Tracking is an event in which the dog is taught to follow the path of a person who has gone ahead of him minutes or hour before. The dog then leads his handler to find the "lost" person. The American Kennel Club awards the title Tracking Dog to dogs that pass tracking tests given by AKC licensed judges.

I had heard about a man in Canada named Glen Johnson who was world renowned in canine olfaction (using the nose to determine information). Angel and I attended several of Glen Johnson's seminars and we worked tirelessly to achieve our goal.

Finally in a Maryland rye field on a cold November day, Angel passed the ultimate exam and became the eighth Miniature Schnauzer in America to earn the coveted "TD." The following summer, Glen invited Angel to be the only small breed dog at a special working olfactory conference and seminar at St. Clair College in Windsor, Ontario. I, being Angel's handler, was invited to come along, too!

After working for five grueling days with 12 handlers and large breed dogs (German Shepherds Dogs, Tervurens, Golden Retrievers, etc.), we began to realize the potential of what was possible to accomplish using a dog's ability to smell odors not perceptible by man.

For example, a dog's scenting ability is better than 15,000 times greater than a human's sense of smell. In other words, dogs smell each individual component of matter whereas man only smells the combines result. Take spaghetti, for example. A dog would smell the sauce as oregano, tomatoes, onions, garlic individually, while man smells the combination and says, "I smell spaghetti sauce."

In the months and years ahead, Angel was trained to detect ovulating cows so the farmer could breed them at the most optimum time. She'd sit on a high platform and sniff each cow as

Brandy Lane Blue Angel, TD, or "Angel" to her friends, owned by author Charlotte Schwartz, exemplifies the versatility and determination of the Miniature Schnauzer.

it passed her on the way to the milking room. Whenever a cow in estrus passed by, Angel would lay down to identify the ovulating cow.

She was trained to locate and indicate drugs and suspect substances such as marijuana. She could also locate and indicate buried plastic that had been buried months before as deep as 12 inches below the ground surface.

At one point in her career, I was working with the Philadelphia Police Department Canine Unit in Pennsylvania. We taught Angel to locate and indicate hidden weapons. She was never allowed to touch the guns. Instead she did a superb job of barking to draw my attention to her "find."

Because of her diminutive size, many law enforcement people didn't believe that a little Miniature Schnauzer could perform such a valuable task as weapons detection. We then documented her expertise on videotape and that dispelled the doubters!

The most exciting job she ever performed was her work with the Police Department of Mt. Holly, New Jersey, in solving the case of a young woman who disappeared during her travels from work to home.

Apparently she had accepted a ride from a fellow worker who had dropped her off several blocks from her home. Bloodhounds had been used a few days later to find the path the woman had taken from the drop-off location. The dogs tracked her to a house (not hers) several blocks away, but the police weren't convinced that the bloodhounds' trail was accurate.

The whole family must be committed to caring for your Miniature Schnauzer.

Angel was called in to verify the trail of the bloodhounds. She began her search for the trail, now five days old, at the drop-off point. The police had earlier identified a shoe print in some dirt alongside the curb and because of its size, believed it to be that of the lost woman. (The woman's mother confirmed that her daughter had worn shoes to work that day with similar type soles and also that her foot size was small like that of the print.)

Angel sniffed the print, circled around the area a bit, then put her nose to the cement sidewalk and began pulling hard. I followed quietly and let her make the decisions about where to go. We walked for two blocks with Angel pulling confidently.

Suddenly, she angled off the sidewalk and up onto a lawn. She sniffed momentarily at a side entrance to the backyard of a house, then turned and led me to the front door. Without hesitating, she turned again, walked to the driveway, and quit sniffing. It was obvious Angel had come to the end of the trail.

The police, a sergeant and two officers, had witnessed Angel's performance from a distance. When she quit scenting, I walked over to them as they stood in the middle of the street in front of the house that Angel had indicated.

"I have no words," admitted the sergeant. "This little dog just confirmed the track of the bloodhounds and now we realize that the young woman was driven away from here by auto. We have a lot more investigating to do in this case. The only resident of this house, a man, knew the girl."

Weeks later, the police found the girl's body and the man in the house was accused of her murder.

In her later years, Angel developed a medical condition of the heart that limited her tracking to short trails and her scenting to easy short-duration work. However, she never lost that Miniature Schnauzer trait of wanting to be in on the action wherever and whenever possible. She was, indeed, a dog with "heart."

For me, living and working with her was an exciting and humbling experience, one you don't easily forget. And one that makes me appreciate how special and unique we all are, for each of us contributes to the total experience of life.

Angel, it seems, was a major contributor. A little dog with a prize-winning personality and General Grant whiskers, she was first and foremost a Miniature Schnauzer.

STANDARD for the Miniature Schnauzer

General **Appearance**—The Miniature Schnauzer is a robust, active dog of terrier type, resembling his larger cousin, the Standard Schnauzer, in general appearance, and of an alert, active disposition. *Faults—Type*—Toyishness, ranginess or coarseness.

Size, Proportion, Substance—*Size*—From 12 to 14 inches. He is sturdily built, nearly square in *proportion* of body length to height with plenty of bone, and without any suggestion of toyishness. *Disqualifications*—Dogs or bitches under 12 inches or over 14 inches.

Head—*Eyes* small, dark brown and deep-set. They are oval in appearance and keen in *expression*. *Faults*—Eyes light and/or large and prominent in appearance. *Ears*—When cropped, the ears are identical in shape and length, with pointed tips. They are in balance with the head and not exaggerated in length. They are set high on the skull and carried perpendicularly at the inner edges, with as little bell as possible along the outer edges. When uncropped, the ears are small and V-shaped, folding close to the skull.

Head strong and rectangular, its width diminishing slightly from ears to eyes, and again to the tip of the nose. The forehead is unwrinkled. The *topskull* is flat and fairly long. The foreface is parallel to the topskull, with a slight stop, and it is at least as long as the topskull. The *muzzle* is strong in proportion to the skull; it ends in a moderately blunt manner, with thick whiskers which accentuate the rectangular shape of the head. *Faults*—Head coarse and cheeky. The *teeth* meet in a *scissors bite*. That is, the upper front teeth overlap the lower front teeth in such a manner that the inner surface of the upper incisors barely touches the outer surface of the lower incisors when the mouth is closed. *Faults*—Bite—Undershot or overshot jaw. Level bite.

Neck, Topline, Body—*Neck* strong and well arched, blending into the shoulders, and with the skin fitting tightly at the throat. *Body* short and deep, with the brisket extending at least to the elbows. Ribs are well sprung and deep, extending well back to a short loin. The underbody does not present a tucked up appearance at the flank. The *backline* is straight; it declines slightly from the withers to the base of the tail. The withers form the highest point

The Miniature Schnauzer is a robust terrier-type dog with an alert active disposition.

of the body. The overall length from chest to buttocks appears to equal the height at the withers. *Faults*—Chest too broad or shallow in brisket. Hollow or roach back.

Tail set high and carried erect. It is docked only long enough to be clearly visible over the backline of the body when the dog is in proper length of coat. *Fault*—Tail set too low.

Forequarters—Forelegs are straight and parallel when viewed from all sides. They have strong pasterns and good bone. They are separated by a fairly deep brisket which precludes a pinched front. The elbows are close, and the ribs spread gradually from the first rib so as to allow space for the elbows to move close to the body. *Fault*—Loose elbows.

The sloping *shoulders* are muscled, yet flat and clean. They are well laid back, so that from the side the tips of the shoulder blades are in a nearly vertical line above the elbow. The tips of the blades are placed closely together. They slope forward and downward at an angulation which permits the maximum forward extension of the forelegs without binding or effort. Both the shoulder blades and upper arms are long, permitting depth of chest at the brisket.

Feet short and round (cat feet) with thick, black pads. The toes are arched and compact.

Hindquarters—The hindquarters have strong-muscled, slanting thighs. They are well bent at the stifles. There is sufficient angulation so that, in stance, the hocks extend beyond the tail. The hindquarters never appear overbuilt or higher than the shoulders. The rear pasterns are short and, in stance, perpendicular to the ground and, when viewed from the rear, are parallel to each other. *Faults*—Sickle hocks, cow hocks, open hocks or bowed hindquarters.

Coat—Double, with hard, wiry, outer coat and close undercoat. The head, neck, ears, chest, tail, and body coat must be plucked. When in show condition, the body coat should be of sufficient length to determine texture. Close covering on neck, ears and skull. Furnishings are fairly thick but not silky. *Faults*—Coat too soft or too smooth and slick in appearance.

Color—The recognized colors are salt and pepper, black and silver and solid black. All colors have uniform skin pigmentation, i.e. no white or pink skin patches shall appear anywhere on the dog.

Salt and Pepper—The typical salt and pepper color of the topcoat results from the combination of black and white banded hairs and solid black and white unbanded hairs, with the banded hairs predominating. Acceptable are all shades of salt and pepper, from light to dark mixtures with tan shadings permissible in the banded or unbanded hair of the topcoat. In salt and pepper dogs, the salt and pepper mixture fades out to light gray or silver white in the eyebrows, whiskers, cheeks, under throat, inside ears, across chest, under tail, leg furnishings, and inside hind legs. It may or may not also fade out on the underbody. However, if so, the lighter underbody hair is not to rise higher on the sides of the body than the front elbows.

Black and Silver—The black and silver generally follows the same pattern as the salt and pepper. The entire salt and pepper section must be black. The black color in the topcoat of the black and silver is a true rich color with black undercoat. The stripped portion is free from any fading or brown tinge and the underbody should be dark.

Black—Black is the only solid color allowed. Ideally, the black color in the topcoat is a true rich glossy solid color with the undercoat being less intense, a soft matting shade of black. This is natural and should not be penalized in any way. The stripped portion is free from any fading or brown tinge. The scissored and clippered areas have lighter shades of black. A small white spot on the chest is permitted, as is an occasional single white hair elsewhere on the body.

The double coat of the hardy Miniature Schnauzer allows him to thrive in any type of weather.

Disqualifications—Color solid white or white striping, patching, or spotting on the colored areas of the dog, except for the small white spot permitted on the chest of the black.

The body coat color in salt and pepper and black and silver dogs fades out to light gray or silver white under the throat and across the chest. Between them there exists a natural body coat color. Any irregular or connecting blaze or white mark in this section is considered a white patch on the body, which is also a disqualification.

Gait—The trot is the gait at which movement is judged. When approaching, the forelegs, with elbows close to the body, move straight forward, neither too close nor too far apart. Going away, the hind legs are straight and travel in the same planes as the forelegs.

Note—*It is generally accepted tht when a full trot is achieved, the rear legs continue to move in the same planes as the forelegs, but a very inward incliination will occur. It begins at the point of the shoulder in front and at the hip joint in the rear. Viewed from the front or rear, the legs are straight from these points to the pads. The degree of inward inclination is almost imperceptible in a Miniature Schnauzer that has correct movement. It does not justify moving close, toeing in, crossing, or moving out at the elbows.*

Viewed from the side, the forelegs have good reach, while the hind legs have strong drive, with good pickup of hocks. The feet turn neither inward nor outward.

Black and silver is one of the most popular colors of the Miniature Schnauzer.

The Miniature Schnauzer's gait should be free, easy, and graceful.

Faults—Single tracking, sidegaiting, paddling in front, or hackney action. Weak rear action.

Temperament—The typical Miniature Schnauzer is alert and spirited, yet obedient to command. He is friendly, intelligent and willing to please. He should never be overaggressive or timid.

DISQUALIFICATIONS

Dogs or bitches under 12 inches or over 14 inches. Color solid white or white striping, patching, or spotting on the colored areas of the dog, except for the small white spot permitted on the chest of the black.

The body coat color in salt and pepper and black and silver dogs fades out to light gray or silver white under the throat and across the chest. Between them there exists a natural body coat color. Any irregular or connecting blaze or white mark in this section is considered a white patch on the body, which is also a disqualification.

Approved January 15, 1991
Effective February 27, 1991

SELECTING Your New Miniature Schnauzer

I f I were allowed just one sentence to offer as advice to the potential puppy buyer, it would be: "Do your homework!" By that I mean investigate the background of the breeds of your interest. Read all the material you can find related to those breeds. Most libraries offer a large selection of books about dogs. *Choosing a Dog for Life* by Andrew DePrisco and James Johnson, published by TFH Publications, is an excellent source of information on dozens of dog breeds.

Go to dog shows in your area. Most shows are advertised in local newspapers, on television, and on the radio. Seek out the people exhibiting the breeds you are interested in and ask lots of questions. Most of all, observe the dogs and how they react to the stress and excitement of crowds and other dogs. Do the dogs appear to be having fun, or do they seem anxious, nervous, or even aggressive toward other dogs and strangers?

Talk to local dog trainers, obedience instructors, and veterinarians and, by all means, listen carefully to what they have to say. They may offer some important clues.

For example, a person may say that a particular breed "isn't fond of strangers" when what they mean is "This is a very aggressive

All puppies are adorable, but make sure the decision to bring a new Mini Schnauzer into your home is a carefully considered one.

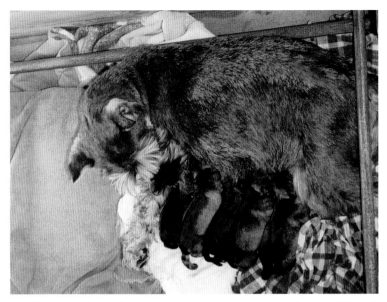

Gretchen, owned by Mark Meeker, nurses her pups. Soon these little guys will be ready to go to their new homes.

breed." "They can be housetrained, but you must be patient" translates to "They're difficult to train."

These traits are not desirable for the average family companion dog and may cause you great heartache if you disregard the warning signs. A protective sense of home and family is present in most breeds, but an excess of aggression toward all but the immediate family can be a lawsuit waiting to happen, so think carefully before you make that final decision.

Furthermore, the mother of an active growing family will not be pleased when she learns she must try to housetrain a dog that doesn't want to cooperate. She has enough to do without spending her days cleaning up after an untrained dog.

Finally, evaluate whether or not you and your loved ones are the right people for a particular breed of dog. If not, this is the time to look at some other breeds.

Veterinarians will be able to tell you what health problems they most often see in the breeds of dog in which you are interested. Some physical problems are easy to manage and cause the dog little or no suffering. Others are more serious, cause a great deal of suffering, and are often life threatening.

Reputable breeders will ensure that the Miniature Schnauzer puppies they produce get the best care possible.

Keep in mind that all the people mentioned above have no financial interest in sharing information with you. Owners, dog show exhibitors, veterinarians, trainers, and instructors are not directly rewarded by giving you advice. You may ultimately seek their professional help, but initially they want only to communicate their findings with genuinely interested parties.

Next talk to breeders. These are the people responsible for producing puppies that are representative of a particular breed of dog. If the puppies grow up to not look and act like the breed they represent, the breeder's credibility is to be questioned.

Reputable breeders care very much about the puppies they produce. They are also proud of their dogs' progeny and only want to see their puppies get into good homes where the dog will flourish and serve as good public relations examples to the world. Talking with breeders is usually not a one-way conversation. Most will gladly answer your questions, volunteer more information than you thought necessary, and show a great deal of interest in you and your reasons for wanting the breed of dog they produce.

In my years as a breeder, I turned away more than one person as a potential puppy buyer. Whether I felt the person was unable to care for the puppy properly or the person and his family were just too unfit to own a dog, I never hesitated to be courteous yet firm in my suggestion for them to either consider a different breed or another type of pet all together.

Perhaps those suggestions did not make me new friends, but at least I felt good knowing that I had saved one of my puppies from a regrettable fate. And, as a breeder, my allegiance to my breed had to come first.

Another excellent source of information is the owners of some of the breeder's puppies. A reputable breeder is more than happy to refer you to some of their puppy buyers. And those buyers are always delighted to have you meet their dogs and share their feelings about their choice of pet.

Your investigation should include looking at photos of some of the dogs produced and shown by the breeder. You'll be able to get a good idea of size, color, and type from these pictures. Ask to see the pedigrees of the sire and dam of the puppies in question. The

Your puppy will get a great head start if his mother and father are healthy and well adjusted. If possible, meet the parents of the pup you are considering.

breeder will also introduce you to the dam of the litter and, if available, the sire as well.

Pedigrees are the history of bloodlines that, combined through generations of breeding, make up the dogs you see today. I always find it fascinating that often a puppy will develop into a carbon copy of a grandparent, so study the pedigrees and get familiar with bloodlines.

You're getting closer to a decision about what breed of dog will best fit into your lifestyle and bring you joy as a companion. There are perfect people and homes for almost every breed of dog. It remains for you to decide what's just the right breed for you.

Next, you need to locate the source of your potential new dog. Sometimes people purchase a dog from a breeder who lives many miles away. This entails a series of letters, phone calls, photos, and much discussion, not to mention that the seller should come highly recommended by someone you know and trust who also knows the seller and his or her reputation within the breed.

Before you are ready to purchase a dog, you have even more details to work out. Let's take a look at some of the additional decisions you'll have to make before you write that check.

What sex of dog you buy will be among your first consideration. Females are usually gentle and enjoy staying close to home. Males are usually more curious and tend to explore the neighborhood more unless controlled. In addition, males are usually larger than females, with heavier bone structure and often more dense and more abundant coats.

Either sex can and should be neutered unless the dog is destined for a show ring and a career of reproduction. Spaying a female and neutering a male has many good results. It makes the dogs mellower, more content to be with family and at home, and easier to control. On the other hand, it does not take away from their protective instincts or ability to function

Intact males are interested in females throughout the year. Intact females usually come in season twice a year for 20 days and thus need to be confined if you don't want them to get pregnant. They can also become finicky and irritable at those times. Lastly, they are extremely interested in male dogs of any breed during periods of estrus.

Breeding puppies should be left to the breeders. Contrary to popular belief, breeding puppies rarely generates large profits for the breeder. The cost of stud fees, the maintenance of a breeding female before, during, and after breeding, and the cost of raising a litter of puppies is extremely high—much higher than most people care to admit!

Worming and vaccinating the puppies before they go to new homes is costly as well. Worming and immunizing puppies against distemper, hepatitis, parainfluenza, parvo and coronavirus before the puppies can be sold is mandatory in many states.

If an emergency arises such as the need for a cesarean delivery, the expenses become astronomical. The cost of the average c-section can run from $350.00 to $500.00. This does not take into account the risk to the mother's life or her future ability to produce puppies and, in most cases, the need for a cesarean cannot be predicted in advance.

PUPPY OR ADULT?

When people think of acquiring a new dog, they most often think of a puppy—one that's between 8 and 12 weeks of age. Although the dictionary defines a puppy as a young dog less than one year of age, I break that down even further.

I consider a puppy to be between the ages of 8 and 20 weeks of age. An adolescent is from 5 to 12 months of age, and an adult is a dog over one year of age. There are advantages and disadvantages to purchasing a dog in each of these categories. You need to know what to expect at each age before you can make a well-informed

Proper socialization with people is an important aspect of raising a puppy. Amanda takes her three-month-old Mini Schnauzer for a walk.

decision about the dog that's going to be a part of your family for many years.

Puppies are like raw clay. You begin with good-quality material and mold it to suit your lifestyle and wishes. Because he hasn't lived long enough to develop bad habits, you can begin teaching the puppy good habits right from the start.

It's fascinating to observe the growth and development of a youngster, whether a human or a dog. Seeing how they learn, mature, and discover the world around them can be extremely exciting and rewarding.

On the minus side, there is teething and chewing, housebreaking, jumping on people and furniture, sometimes excessive barking, and digging with which to contend. You should plan on crate training your puppy and be prepared to take him outdoors frequently until his urinary system is fully developed at about six months of age. This means getting up several times during the night and serving breakfast at six in the morning! And little puppies need to be fed three times a day.

Because they're teething and often have aching gums, little puppies love to chew on soft things, especially your hands and ankles. If you have toddlers or tiny babies in the home, Miniature Schnauzer puppies can be a problem if they're in the same stages of development as the human babies.

If you do not have the time or desire to train a young puppy, an older Miniature Schnauzer may be the best addition to your family.

In addition, young puppies, like young children, must be supervised constantly when they're not sleeping or safe in their crates. Failure to accept this fact can result in drastic results that can bring harm to the puppies as well as your personal property.

Little puppies can get sat on by toddlers and sometimes injured in the process. Further, toddlers don't always understand your attempts to train the puppy and frequently undo whatever it is you're trying to accomplish. Think about all these things before you decide on the age of the dog you'll buy.

Adolescent dogs have the early housetraining behind them and are usually pretty reliable when it comes to not having accidents in the house. Although there are still some developmental stages to go through, the adolescent usually understands what "no" means. He chews less because his permanent front teeth are in, but still faces the emergence of molars that often cause some serious chewing on hard items. If you realize this, you can provide hard bones for chewing and teach him not to use your coffee table legs as chew toys.

The adolescent is still young enough to form a bond with you if you make an effort. He is eager to participate in your lifestyle yet occasionally needs reminders to use good manners. You'll be able to witness the transformation from gangly teenager with long spindly legs that seem to go in every direction at once to graceful adult. All these stages of development are exciting to observe and participate in.

Whether you choose a baby or an adolescent puppy, you should plan on taking the dog to an obedience class for some basic training. Not only will he learn good manners and simple commands such as sit, stay, down, and come, but he will build that bond with you as his master. This is the foundation from which all you do together for the rest of his life will come. It's worth the time and effort!

Now let's consider purchasing an adult dog. First, you need to know that adults for sale are rare compared to the availability of puppies. Occasionally you may see an advertisement in a newspaper for an adult, but you must seriously question the reasons why this dog is for sale. Sometimes people sell adults because of behavior problems that you will not be able to correct. In this case, you'll be stuck with someone else's problem!

Once in a while a reputable breeder will offer to sell an adult because the dog's show career has ended, possibly because of age or physical problems. The breeder will usually spay or neuter the dog and look for a good home in which to place him as a pet.

With an adult dog, there are no growing problems to face, but you must be prepared to allow the dog enough time to adjust to his new home with you. This requires a lot of patience on your part, but it can be most rewarding.

Adult dogs are ideal purchases for older people with limited physical abilities and stamina. Providing the dog is well mannered, the adult dog can better fit into a quieter slower lifestyle than a young puppy.

Young families with active children do not make ideal homes for older dogs if the dog has had no prior experiences with growing children and all that it implies. If, however, an adult dog is coming from an active family that included young children, the dog will likely learn to love his new young masters and fit in well. It will be up to you to determine whether or not your home situation is similar to that from which the adult is coming.

The cost of an adult dog is often much less than it is for a puppy or adolescent. The purpose in placing an adult dog is usually for the dog's benefit, so price is rarely a consideration. The bottom line that the breeder will be looking at is whether or not her adult dog will fit well into your home and family unit.

SOCIALIZATION

Regardless of the age of dog you choose to purchase, one of the most important factors in choosing a new dog is how you perceive that dog when you first meet him and spend some time getting to know him. We've all heard the story about the person who was searching for a dog, found one and, upon meeting the animal, discovered that he and the dog were made for each other.

However, a dog of any age, even a puppy, that runs from you, hides in a corner, or in any way acts frightened of your presence is not an ideal candidate no matter how appealing he may look. The key to preventing this problem of shyness in the first place is socialization, and socialization must begin with the breeder long before you ever meet the dog.

As a matter of fact, the older a dog is before socialization begins, the more difficult it is for the dog to adjust to new situations and surroundings. Some dogs, deprived of early socialization, are never able to adjust to new homes and people and are doomed to live out their lives in their original home, never knowing how wonderful and full life can be.

Your new Miniature Schnauzer should meet as many different people as possible, especially children. The more people he meets, the better socialized he will become.

Start to socialize a puppy when he is four or five weeks of age by letting family members and friends hold and play with him. He should be subjected to a wide variety of situations and environments, such as a backyard, a kitchen, a park, a ride in the car just for fun, a visit to meet children, and other pets. In other words, the young puppy is exposed to a cross section of life as he will know it when he becomes an adult.

Once the puppy is settled in his new home, the same procedure must be repeated regularly in new surroundings with all new people and pets. If this socialization is approached on a basis of fun and is rewarded with positive attention, the puppy's confidence level will grow so he can cope with life and all it has to offer.

That is one of the major advantages to puppy kindergarten and beginner's training classes. The exposure to new dogs, people, and experiences assures a well-balanced adult who is sure of himself and his family.

If you're considering an adolescent, make sure that he has been properly and adequately socialized during his formative months (between two and five months of age). You can tell if this is so by observing how he handles meeting you and your family.

Look for the dog, either puppy or adult, who accepts you and appears interested in interacting with you. Needless to say, a dog

As long as they are properly introduced, your Mini Schnauzer should get along famously with other pets.

Socialization with other dogs is necessary for a well-adjusted pet. Mini Schnauzer Maxwell hangs out with Bunny, his Shetland Sheepdog friend.

that shows signs of little or no socialization skills should not be considered for purchase.

For example, a shy fearful Miniature Schnauzer, whether puppy or adult, may feel threatened when approached and may resort to biting. Regardless of the reason for biting, a bite is a bite and must be considered a serious matter. Consequently, never consider taking a dog into your life that shows signs of shyness.

As a matter of fact, signs of shyness are so undesirable that in the Standard of Perfection for most breeds, the American Kennel Club labels this trait a major fault. Do not be fooled into thinking it will go away with time. I have known a number of people who have taken non-socialized dogs into their homes because they felt sorry for them. They wanted to work with the dogs and give them a good life. This, however, was never accomplished and frequently ended when the dog either ran away or bit someone and was euthenized as a final solution. In all those cases, the people involved were heartbroken when they realized they could not change behavioral patterns that had been formed in the developmental stages of the dog's life.

In short, socialization, or the lack of it, serves to determine the path the dog's behavior will follow for his entire life. That being the case, which incidentally has been proven by scientific studies, socialization effects you as much as the dog.

Important Papers

Let's address the matter of kennel clubs, registrations, pedigrees, and what they mean to you. Kennel clubs are registering bodies for purebred dogs. In addition, they maintain records such as championship titles, sporting event degrees, and offspring produced by individual dogs registered with them.

For example, when an American Kennel Club (AKC) registered sire (father) and dam (mother) produce a litter of puppies, the breeder registers the litter's birth with the AKC. Each puppy in that litter is then given an individual registration application form that goes with the puppy to the new owner.

In a recent public information ad, the American Kennel Club wrote, "If you buy a purebred dog that you are told is eligible for registration with the American Kennel Club, you are entitled to receive from the seller an application form that will enable you to register your dog.

"If the seller cannot give you the application, you should demand and receive full identification of your dog in writing, signed by the seller, consisting of the breed, the registered names and individual registration numbers of your dog's sire and dam, your dog's date of birth, the names of its breeder and, if available, its AKC litter number. Don't be misled by promises of 'papers' later."

The new owner then selects a name for his puppy and registers that name with the AKC which, in turn, gives the puppy his own individual registration number. That number stays with the dog for life. The number is also used to trace the ancestors of the dog and create a pedigree, or genealogical record. The pedigree will tell you the names of any given dog's parents, grandparents, great-grandparents, etc.

If you purchase a puppy whose sire and dam are not known, but you believe him to be a purebred dog, you may apply to the AKC for an ILP number. An Indefinite Listing Privilege number allows you to exhibit the dog in AKC sporting events and earn titles. However, a dog with an ILP may not be exhibited in the conformation ring or earn a breed Championship title.

To obtain an ILP number, write to the AKC for an application form. They will probably ask for pictures of your dog and written statements from knowledgeable experts who testify that, in their opinions, your dog is pure bred. If, after investigating your claim, the AKC agrees that your dog is a pure breed, they will issue a number and send you a certificate to that effect. From then on you may participate in AKC dog activities for fun.

SOURCES

Once your investigation of various breeds of dogs is complete and, provided you've decided a Miniature Schnauzer is for you, there are some other matters that need your attention. One of them is the source of your new dog.

If you plan to purchase an adolescent or adult dog, there are limited choices. But if you're looking for a puppy, then you need to find breeders who have puppies for sale.

When choosing a puppy, take a hard look first at the home or kennel. Is the atmosphere chaotic or orderly? Do the adult dogs

Well-trained and socialized Miniature Schnauzers can participate in any activity. Mandy (as a witch) and BB (as a vampire) get ready for Halloween.

appear friendly and healthy? Does the breeder appear knowledgeable about his or her breed? Is he or she concerned about the welfare of the puppies and their future homes?

Next look at the whole litter and their living quarters. Their sleeping and play areas should be clean and free of unpleasant odors. If the puppies are using newspaper for elimination, it should be changed as needed. If they're outdoors, their elimination area should show signs of being frequent cleaned up.

If possible, observe the puppies eating a meal and see how they react to each other. Look for puppies that eat eagerly and do not act aggressively toward littermates. Overprotectiveness of food at this early age may signal problems in the adult dog.

Do the puppies appear active and healthy? They should have bright eyes with no discharge coming from them. Their stools should show no signs of diarrhea. Their coats will be fluffy and full and should be clean and free of parasites such as fleas and ticks.

As your eyes begin to focus on certain puppies in the litter, concentrate on their behavior, for it often predicts what they will be like as adults. For example, the bully of the litter may grow up to become a very dominant individual that can sometimes be difficult

When choosing a puppy, make sure the dam and litter are kept in a clean area and that all the pups look healthy and well cared for.

to control. The runt, or smallest one, may not fit your criteria for a busy lifestyle. He may grow up to be very timid or he may develop in the opposite direction and become the tyrant of the neighborhood.

A friendly, outgoing, yet not hyperactive puppy begins life with a lot going for him.

Socialization with littermates is important for good relationships with other dogs later in life.

He should be curious and alert, have a bright intelligence in his expression, and be eager to hang around people.

Among dog folk there is an old saying that there are basically two kinds of dogs—"dog" dogs and "people" dogs. The "dog" dogs are happiest when they're with their own kind and will spend their lives attempting to socialize with other dogs. Human companionship is secondary to them.

"People" dogs are more content to be with you. They accept other dogs, but prefer the company of their owners and will almost always choose you over other pets. This is the type of dog who will be eager to learn, anxious to please, and happy doing things with you all his life.

SHOW QUALITY OR PET?

If you are interested in exhibiting in the breed ring, you must not only consider temperament, but you must look at the puppy with an eye to what he'll look like as an adult.

Here's where the help of the breeder is paramount. Nobody can accurately predict how a puppy will turn out, but the breeder, particularly if he or she has a history of raising good-quality show dogs, is in a position to assist you in making the best choice. For example, the breeder will have a good idea of the puppy's eventual size, as well as coat color and type.

The price of a show puppy will probably be a lot more than the price of a puppy destined for a pet home. After all, the show dog will be shown at great cost in time, training, and money, and ultimately bred to contribute more fine specimens to the breed in years to come. For example, if and when your puppy grows up to become a champion, the price you can demand for the stud fee of a male or the puppies of a female will be much higher than the price for puppies from pet stock.

On the other hand, you can purchase a pet-quality puppy out of the same litter from which a show-quality puppy comes. The difference in show and pet quality is often very small and noticeable only to trained experts.

The pet puppy, however, has come from the same parents, has had the same quality upbringing, and has received the same socialization and start in life that his show-quality littermate has. The fact that the show puppy may have the potential for a thicker coat, a longer muzzle, or a heavier bone as an adult will not affect the pet-quality puppy you choose. And you will be benefiting from the care and attention the entire litter received before, during, and after birth.

In addition, you will still be able to train and exhibit your dog in obedience trials and earn titles for your dog. The sport of obedience is exciting and rewarding and is open to all purebred dogs, regardless of whether or not they are show quality or sexually altered.

All Mini Schnauzers are adorable, but when choosing a show-quality puppy, you must seriously consider his conformation.

Miniature Schnauzer Sercateps Midnite Confessions, owned by Mary Grundy.

In fact, when you review the puppy's pedigree, you may see dogs listed with CD, CDX, UD, or UDX following their names. These obedience titles are significant in demonstrating the willingness and capability of those individuals to work with their owners. To document this, the dogs have been exhibited at obedience trials, thereby proving their value as companion animals.

The initials TD and TDX after a dog's name indicate that dog has earned an AKC Tracking Dog or Tracking Dog Excellent title. Tracking teaches a dog to use his nose to follow the path of someone who has gone ahead of him minutes or hours before. Whether a pet or show dog, he has established himself as a hearty individual who has proved he is worthy for more things than just fun and entertainment.

If you're purchasing a puppy from a local hobby breeder who has bred a litter of puppies for the first time, you need to be particularly careful in your selection. First, the mother of the litter has no record of what she produces in size, coat color, temperament, etc. Ask the owner where the dam came from—that information could be a clue as to what you can expect from her puppies.

If the female was bred to a local pet male, you may want to visit his home and meet him. Study his behavior and observe his appearance and general physical condition, as well as his disposition. If you don't like the parents, don't buy the puppy.

Perhaps, if you do your homework now, you may be as fortunate as I was many years ago when I purchased a female Miniature Schnauzer named Brandy from a first-time hobby breeder. Brandy's dam had been bred to a champion and the owner of the female was guided in her breeding program by reputable breeders with years of experience.

Brandy ultimately grew up to be a fine specimen of the breed with correct temperament. When she was two years old, I bred her to a champion and she produced four puppies. For me, that was the beginning of 17 years of breeding, showing, and training Miniature Schnauzers.

Coat and Color

Now let's focus our attention on Miniature Schnauzer puppy coats and colors. Unlike some breeds of dog that are born with the exact color as their parents, Miniature Schnauzers are not. Most of them are born black with shadings of tan, beige, or brown flanks, ears, and chins. As they grow, these shading will change to white or silver to form what we refer to as the furnishings. Little spots above their eyes can also be light in color and these, of course, will ultimately become their eyebrows.

In the case of solid black Miniature Schnauzers, the puppies are born solid black with black skin as well. As stated earlier, they are permitted to have a small white spot on their chest and, at birth, this area may appear tan in color.

The hair on all puppies will be short and lay close to the skin. As the weeks go by, this hair grows in length, and by the time they're six weeks of age it will begin to look straggly and unkempt. Brushing will improve their appearance only temporarily.

Those shaded areas will begin to change to light gray, silver, or white, and by the time the puppies are eight weeks of age, the furnishings will be clearly defined. In black Miniature Schnauzers, the coat grows and the straggly look appears, but the furnishings remain solid black. The white spot on the chest may appear to disappear, but if you push the chest hair aside, you'll see that the spot is still there—it's just hidden by the lengthening coat.

Because Miniature Schnauzers require a great deal of grooming, the breeder will begin working with the puppy as early as four weeks

When choosing a Miniature Schnauzer, coat color is a personal preference. Maxwell and Abbey are salt and peppers, and Black Jack has a black coat.

If you introduce your Miniature Schnauzer to grooming procedures when he is young, it will become a pleasurable experience for both of you.

A Miniature Schnauzer puppy, once groomed, should look like his adult relatives, only smaller.

of age. Don't forget this is a lifelong necessity and the earlier the pup learns to accept grooming, the easier it will be for all concerned.

The process of daily brushing will pull out a lot of that early coat, so by the time the puppy gets his first full grooming, he is already accustomed to standing on a grooming table and having someone work on him. He will have his toenails clipped, his ears cleaned, and possibly the hair around his rear end scissored short for hygienic purposes. (Puppies do tend to get pretty messy with their bathroom habits before they learn how to void without soiling themselves!)

At about seven or eight weeks of age, the puppy will experience his first full grooming session. I call this his "butterfly moment." With clippers in hand, the groomer quickly trims away all that scraggly long hair over the head, neck, and body of the puppy. The ears are shaved close, the underbody is clipped, and the rump is contoured to accent the white or silver hair beneath the tail.

Scissors snip away excess hair on the sides of the head and sculpt the eyebrows and short little whiskers. Lighter leg hairs are trimmed and blended into the upper body to create a continuous line from straight strong legs to square body. Finally, the hair around the feet is rounded and, almost like magic, the metamorphosis is complete.

Voila! Now what you see is a tiny version of an adult Miniature Schnauzer. From this moment on, as the weeks and months pass, the dog will continue to grow hair and have it groomed again and again. The world will never know that once upon a time when he was eight weeks old, he was transformed from an ugly duckling into a handsome terrier in the space of a few minutes!

Specific Health Problems of the Miniature Schnauzer

Many breeds of dogs have certain health problems common to their breed. But before we address specific problems, it's important to investigate the general health of the puppies and both parents. Seeing the parents of the pup you are considering in person can tell a lot about their overall condition. How they look and act offers strong hints into their physical condition.

While visiting the parents, discuss with the owners any possible hereditary physical problems they might have. Remember that hereditary means "capable of genetically passing on to the offspring," so making certain that the parents do not have these types of problems goes a long way toward assuring that the puppies will not have them either.

Before you decide to bring a Miniature Schnauzer into your life, do your homework and make sure this is the right breed for you and your family.

A basketful of love and affection are in store for you and your Miniature Schnauzer puppy.

Certain Miniature Schnauzer bloodlines are known to have several health problems that you might ask about. Some of them are serious and need to be avoided.

Urinary tract problems, kidney disease, and some skin conditions occur in the breed. Eye problems such as progressive retinal atrophy (PRA), retinal degeneration, and juvenile cataracts can be hereditary and can cause blindness. Legg-Perthes disease, liver defects, and von Willebrand's disease have also been found in Miniature Schnauzers.

These problems can be avoided by careful selection. All it takes is some time and inquiry to determine that the puppy under your consideration is free of genetic health problems. A healthy happy puppy is worth the extra effort you devote to finding him.

There are some physical problems that occur in puppies of all breeds and are not hereditary. Intestinal parasites, for example, are common among puppies and easily corrected by your veterinarian. Diarrhea is often caused by foreign objects entering the digestive system or by an improper diet.

Like little children, puppies frequently put anything they find into their mouths. Often they swallow the objects. Grass, small sticks, and stones, even socks and tiny toys that are found around the home are just some of the objects ingested by puppies of all breeds.

The decision to bring a dog into your home and life is not a decision to be made lightly. The choice you make must be an informed intelligent one. I said it before and I will say it again—for the best chance at getting a Miniature Schnauzer that will become a great companion, *do your homework!*

CARING for Your Miniature Schnauzer

The big day is about to arrive. You've done your homework, you've decided that a Miniature Schnauzer is the perfect breed for you, and you've found just the right puppy that makes your heart beat faster. What next? Before you introduce the new member of your family into your home, let's go over some of the things you'll need to provide before you actually get the puppy. As before, if you make appropriate arrangements now, you and the puppy will experience an easy transition from birth environment to new home. The big day and the weeks that follow will be smooth and pleasant for all concerned.

Housing will be the most immediate need with which you'll be faced. Whether you've chosen a tiny ball of fluff at eight weeks of age or an older dog, you should know exactly where and how the dog will be contained in your home once you get him there. Simply turning a new puppy loose to wander around the house is asking for trouble with a capital "T!"

Crate training is the best way to provide comfort and safety for your new Mini Schnauzer puppy.

Feeding your Miniature Schnauzer a well-balanced meal will help maintain his health.

Crate training is the optimum way of providing comfort and safety for your puppy. Contrary to what some people believe, crate training is not inhumane. If he hasn't been crate trained by the breeder, the puppy may object at first, but with proper training and patience on your part, he'll soon learn to love his crate. Crate training is humane and gives the puppy an immediate sense of security.

A dog in the wild, for example, makes a small, dark den for himself where he can sleep, rest, and be safe from predators and enemies. The area, often in soft dirt or in a riverbank beneath the roots of a large tree, usually has a small entranceway. The inside is just large enough for him to lie down and curl into a ball and sleep. The ceiling is often so low that he can barely stand up, yet he seeks out his den whenever he feels tired or anxious.

The crate provides security for you and your home as much as for your puppy. Left free to wander, the puppy will soon get into trouble when he discovers electric cords, soft furniture to chew, and carpets to shred. In addition to that, the puppy will likely eliminate wherever he happens to be when the urge to urinate or defecate hits him. Soon your home will become a smelly disheveled disaster area and you'll either be looking for a new home for the puppy or you'll resort to physical punishment. That will only make the puppy resent and distrust you and thus destroy any hope of the two of you building a bond together.

By providing structured and supervised living quarters, your puppy will feel secure and make a positive transition to his new lifestyle, and you'll enjoy knowing he's out of harm's way.

I have helped thousands of people over the years to crate train their puppies. All of them have told me later that they don't know how they could have managed without the positive aspects of crate training. Remarked one gentleman, "My dog sees his crate as a safe den and frequently seeks it out when he's tired or needs some time out from our busy family activities." This man, incidentally, initially told me that he considered crate training to be "cruel confinement." But the puppy and his crate soon changed the man's opinion on the matter!

FEEDING

Talk to the breeder and get a list of the kinds and brands of food the puppy has been fed. Dogs have very sensitive digestive systems, so changing brands abruptly will usually cause diarrhea and great discomfort to the puppy, to say nothing of the extra cleanup work for you.

Also record the number of meals per day that the puppy has been eating and the times of day he's eaten. Try to maintain this schedule

Pick a good-quality dog food that is nutritionally adequate and appropriate for your dog's stage of life. Puppies need a growth formula.

A puppy receives his first nutrients from nursing, but after he is weaned, it is up to you, the owner, to provide him with his nutritional requirements.

for at least two weeks after you get him. Changing his environment and being separated from his dam and siblings is traumatic enough—he does not need the added physical stress.

Water should also be available at times during the day when he's out of his crate. At night, however, it's wise to restrict water consumption to a few sips after the last meal of the day. You and the puppy will not want to get up too many times during the night!

Never feed a puppy from your plate or the dinner table. It may be cute when he's a tiny baby, but cute turns to nuisance when he becomes an adult. Right from day one he needs to know that his meal comes from his bowl, not yours. First, you'll never know exactly how much and when a puppy is eating. Second, food left out can spoil quickly in warm temperatures, making your dog sick. And third, you miss seeing any subtle hints that the puppy is not feeling well when he nibbles halfheartedly.

When you feed on a regular schedule, you can observe the puppy eating, and you will be able to monitor the puppy's general health. Thus, when problems occur, you will notice the onset of trouble before it becomes serious.

When feeding puppies and adults, put down the food bowl and leave it alone for 15 minutes. At the end of that time, remove the bowl and offer no more food until the next scheduled meal. Dogs quickly figure out that when the food bowl is presented, they'd better get right to it before you take it away. There is no chance for attracting unwanted pests in the kitchen or for developing picky eaters this way, as well.

Cool clean water should be available to your Miniature Schnauzer at all times.

EXERCISE

There are several kinds of exercises we need to address. Exercising for elimination, for muscle building and coordination skills, for fun and bonding, and for learning are all important to help your puppy grow.

Give your dog plenty of safe toys to satisfy his desire to chew and keep his teeth and gums healthy.

Elimination exercising should be limited to specific areas so the puppy learns that your command "Let's go out!" (or whatever phrase you care to use) along with visiting the same area each time, helps him to associate voiding with your command. Taking him for long walks through the neighborhood is not the way to teach house-training, as the puppy has so much to investigate that eliminating becomes

Proper exercise and plenty of play time will help form a close bond between owner and dog.

lost in the adventure of exploring the neighborhood. Then, when he gets back in the house, he suddenly remembers he has to go and another accident happens.

Once the puppy is housebroken, he can be offered opportunities to discover his neighborhood. By then his body will also be strong enough to benefit from extended exercising. Muscle building and coordination skills can be developed in the very young puppy with simple games of fetch played indoors. Because his bones are not fully grown and hardened, excessive exercising is dangerous and may cause physical problems later in life.

For the eight-week-old puppy, just following you around the kitchen and family room will soon tire him out and he'll collapse into a deep sleep for anywhere from 10 to 30 minutes. As the puppy grows, his capacity for exercise will increase and you'll see his need for more and more exercise grow with him.

If there are young children in the family, don't allow them to overdo play and exercise with the puppy. You should always be there to supervise any interaction between children and dog. Teaching children how to treat the puppy and teaching the puppy how to act with children is all part of your responsibility when raising them both.

One trick I developed years ago with children was to teach the "sit and hold" habit. Rather than let little children hold puppies when they were standing up, I taught the kids to sit on the floor when they wanted to hold a puppy. That way, if the puppy wriggled out of their arms, the puppy wouldn't have far to fall to the floor, thus preventing potentially serious accidents.

Taking the puppy to different environments, such as a shopping center, park, beach, or wooded trail not only serves to socialize the puppy but also gives him plenty of exercise to strengthen his developing muscles. In addition, it serves to help you and the puppy build a strong bond of loyalty to each other.

Finally, exercising as a form of learning brings great pleasure to both teacher (you) and student (puppy). Playing hide-and-seek in the house or a fenced backyard is good exercise for the puppy and at the same time, he learns to come to you for praise and a treat.

Teaching Miniature Schnauzers to fetch is fun and easy. Use a soft toy such as one of the simulated lamb's wool toys or Nylabone® chew toys. Interest the puppy in getting it by wiggling it on the floor in front of him. When his interest is keen, toss it a few feet away as you say "Get it!" When he runs out to pick it up, say "Good.boy! Bring it here." It won't be long before he gets the idea that if he brings it back to you, you'll toss it again. Always praise him lavishly when he picks up and carries the toy.

To ensure complete and proper bone development, don't allow puppies under one year of age to jump. However, any other active game can encourage muscle development and be fun for the puppy. Just keep the games short and lively.

Toys

Toys are an important part of puppy development for several reasons. First, every infant, whether human or animal, needs to learn to play because play is really practice for handling life situations in adulthood.

Play fighting, play hunting, play mating, play stalking, play grooming, and power playing are nature's way of teaching the young puppy how to conduct himself when he grows up. It provides practical lessons in how to interact with his own kind and succeed.

Play also provides an opportunity for muscle development. Running, chasing, catching, climbing, and similar activities serve to strengthen growing bodies. Nylabones® and Gumabones® are excellent toys for these activities.

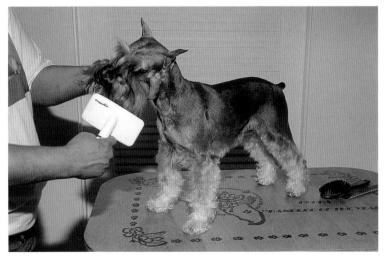

A well-groomed dog is a happy dog. Brush your dog's coat on a regular basis.

Second, playing with you is extremely beneficial to the bond you and the dog build together. Playing reinforces the idea that he is most certainly a vital member of your pack.

When you control the games—begin and end the games at your discretion, not the puppy's—it sends a message to the puppy that you are the pack leader. That in itself teaches him to respect you, and makes learning other behaviors more meaningful.

Finally, playing with other people is important, too. He learns to play gently with children and older folks. He learns to inhibit his bite reflex and use his mouth in a gentle manner. He learns body control and how to use his energy efficiently. He learns self control and all about the rewards it brings through attention and affection. We see then that toys and playing are paramount to raising a well-rounded individual with good physical and mental skills that will serve him well for life.

GROOMING

All dogs need to be groomed regularly; Miniature Schnauzers more so than most. Because they do not shed, the owner has two options from which to choose that will meet that need. The dog can be groomed by clipping the hair or plucking the hair.

As stated earlier, only those individuals destined for the show ring need hand plucking. Stripping the hair will develop the necessary harsh wiry coat required for the show ring. This method, however, is not for the pet Miniature Schnauzer.

Because they do not shed, Miniature Schnauzers need regular grooming to look their best.

Hand plucking requires a constant regimen of weekly, if not daily, attention. It involves removing the old coat in a specific pattern so that, when shown, the coat will appear to be the same length all over the body, with the exception of the head and neck area, which should be short and close to the skin. If left ungroomed, the Miniature Schnauzer would have a coat that was long, shaggy, and unkempt.

Fortunately for pet dogs, electric clippers can do a superb grooming job in a very short time. It will need repeating

Grooming sessions are a great way to spend quality time with your dog, as well as keep on top of any skin or coat problems.

about every eight weeks throughout the dog's life. The cost of pet grooming is minimal compared to show plucking. The only change to the coat when the dog is clipped is that the coat will eventually have a soft, rather than wiry, feel to it.

Most pet owners don't seem to mind the soft coat. They simply want their dogs to be well groomed and look smart at all times. There is, however, a third alternative to pet grooming I'd like to mention—the owner-groomed dog. Once the initial expense of buying the necessary equipment is satisfied, the cost of grooming falls to almost nothing. Buying shampoo and having clipper blades sharpened are the biggest expenses. The most important factor to consider when a person decides to groom his own Miniature Schnauzer is commitment. You must ask yourself if you are willing to groom the dog on a regular basis throughout the dog's lifetime.

Complete grooming includes not only clipping the body coat, but trimming the leg and head furnishing, trimming toenails, keeping the ears free of hair growth, bathing, drying, and scissoring. It can take several hours for the novice groomer to complete a Miniature Schnauzer's coat. The professional can accomplish the same amount of work in about an hour.

Most owners find a middle-of-the-road approach the most practical and pleasant for all concerned. They have the dog professionally groomed every six to eight weeks and they bath and brush the dog weekly in between. That way they don't have to learn how to clipper a coat, clean ears, or trim toenails. The consequence? The dog looks good at all times and the owner saves the expense of between-grooming bathing and brushing by a professional. It's sort of like having the best of both worlds.

If you wish to learn how to groom your own Miniature Schnauzer, there are courses you can take as well as books you can read on the subject. Additionally, some professional groomers will, for a fee, teach you how to do it yourself. But remember if you use your own Miniature Schnauzer in the lessons, it will take you many months to become proficient at grooming, since you'll only have one chance every six to eight weeks to practice the art of clipping and scissoring.

Ideally, your new Miniature Schnauzer puppy should come to you having been groomed at least once by the breeder or seller. The body coat will be clipped short, the little beard and eyebrows trimmed, and leg furnishings will be blended into the body coat. The dog will be bathed, ears cleaned and free of hair, toenails trimmed, etc.

That first experience on a grooming table is an important one for the puppy. It will introduce him to the sound and feel of being

A proper diet of a nutritious dog food, as well as plenty of water, will keep your dog's coat in top condition.

groomed, something he must accept for the rest of his life. Grooming is to a groomable breed as visiting the dentist is to us—unavoidable.

The reputable and experienced breeder knows that introducing a puppy to grooming must be done early in life and

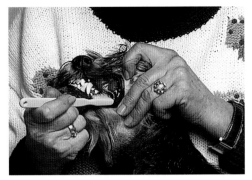

Good oral hygiene is important to the overall health of your Miniature Schnauzer.

continued on a regular basis. It's simply a part of life and it's the breeder responsibility to take the first step in the introduction. If done properly, the puppy will accept the process with tolerance and grace.

Once you bring the puppy into your life, you can continue this regimen by brushing the puppy everyday. When you finish, it's a good idea to celebrate the puppy's good behavior on the grooming table by rewarding him with a biscuit or treat and enthusiastic praises.

Before deciding whether or not to groom your own Miniature Schnauzer, it will behoove you to carefully study photographs of some well-groomed dogs, including those in pet clips as well as the wiry show styles. Note how the shorter body coats blend smoothly into the longer leg furnishings. There is no sharp demarkation between short and long hair. Note the shape and length of eyebrows, beard, and hair around the feet. This book contains many fine examples.

Notice also how the very short head and neck hair blends into the top and sides of the longer body coat. Clipping the body is easy. Blending rear, head, and neck hair into the body is tricky. It will take you many grooming sessions before you become proficient at getting that all-over smooth look, so be patient with yourself.

Just remember that hair grows. If you make a mistake, it will soon grow out and you can try again. Be careful around the face and rear so that you don't mistakenly cut the dog's skin while learning to use the clippers.

Below I have divided the process of grooming into four steps: brushing, bathing, clipping, and scissoring. I must stress here that

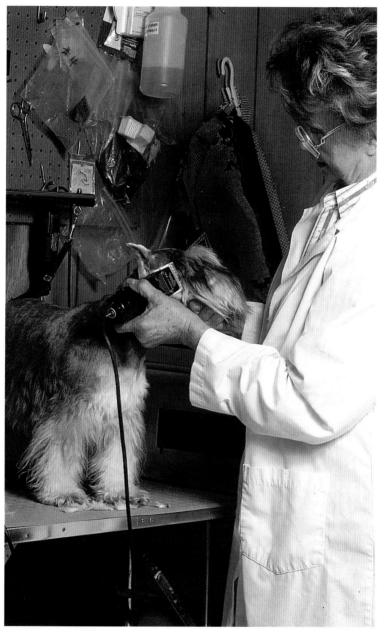

Miniature Schnauzers that compete in conformation will need to have their coat professionally trimmed and kept in show condition.

there is no room in this book for detailed instructions on clipping and scissoring. (That must be left to whole volumes on the subject!) I do give specific instructions on bathing and brushing, however. I have also included a complete list of equipment needed to properly groom the Miniature Schnauzer.

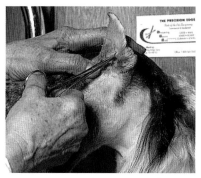

Your Miniature Schnauzer's ears should be clean, neat, and free of waxy build up.

Equipment

1. A grooming table or non-slip surface at table or counter height. Never groom the dog on the floor. Let him learn right from the start that grooming is business and he must stand still and behave whenever he's on the grooming table.

2. A pin brush and a slicker brush. The pin brush is for brushing long hair and the slicker is used for removing tiny knots and larger mats.

3. A metal comb will remove burrs and foreign material from the furnishings and beard.

4. Two pairs of haircutting scissors—the larger one for trimming leg furnishings and the smaller one for working around the head and feet. Scissors can also be used to cut up large mats that can then be brushed out with a slicker.

5. A pair of thinning shears is essential for blending hair from different lengths into that finished look.

6. A pair of good-quality sharp nail trimmers and a styptic pencil (to stop bleeding nails that you may have cut too short).

7. A pair of tweezers for pulling hair from inside the ears. Cotton balls and plain rubbing alcohol are used for cleaning the ears once they are free of hair.

8. Shampoo for bathing and towels for rough drying.

9. Clipping equipment further discussed under *clipping*

10. A hair dryer with a "low" setting. The hand-held type is the easiest to use.

Because the Miniature Schnauzer wears a short body coat, little brushing is necessary over the body. The long thick hair of the whiskers must be brushed out gently. Be cautious around the eyes.

Hold the dog's head still by grasping the beard under the chin firmly. Brush the beard from up near the eyes toward the tip of the nose and beyond.

When brushing the legs, hold the dog's foot in one hand and brush the leg hair in long, slow strokes from the feet upward toward the body. If you brush from the top of the leg downward, you're likely to cover only the outside or top layer and miss the tiny knots and foreign matter in the leg hair. It's those tiny knots and pieces of debris such as grass clippings that can grow into huge mats that can cause the dog severe discomfort and future skin problems.

When one leg is completely brushed, test your work by running the comb gently through the hair from the top of the leg to the feet. Any knots you missed will stop the comb and you can go back and re-brush that area to free up every strand of hair.

Always brush the coat before bathing the dog. If you reserve the procedure, the knots in the coat will become even worse when they get wet. Actually, that means you'll have to brush the dog twice, once before bathing and once again after he's dry. However, the second brushing will be quick and easy if you did a good job the first time.

With proper and patient training, cooperation from the dog, and experience in handling the coat and the brush simultaneously, you'll find that you can brush out a Miniature Schnauzer in just a few

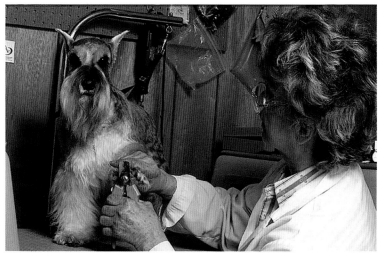

Your Miniature Schnauzer's feet must be inspected regularly for injuries and his toenails kept short to prevent any tearing or discomfort.

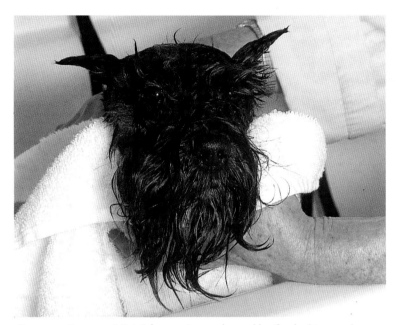

Be sure to rinse your Mini Schnauzer's coat thoroughly after bathing, as shampoo residue can irritate the skin.

minutes. And if you do as I do and reward the dog with a treat when the job is done, your dog will come running to you when he hears, "It's brush-out time!"

The secret to brushing the coat of a dog is to do it often and regularly. Never allow tiny knots to become huge masses of tangled hair. That way the dog will never experience the pain of having you pull out great chunks of his coat. Further, the skin beneath those masses will not have an opportunity to develop open sores and infection.

Bathing

When bathing the Miniature Schnauzer, make it fun for the dog and he'll soon learn to love bath time. Whenever I begin raising a puppy, I teach the dog that bath time is fun and is always followed by a special treat such as a biscuit or a piece of cheese. As adults, my dogs come running every time they hear me say "It's bath time!"

Use a regular dog shampoo and warm water when you bathe your Miniature Schnauzer. Wet the dog down, apply shampoo, and rub it into a lather the same way you shampoo your own hair.

Rinse thoroughly with warm water and follow that with a brisk towel drying.

The final drying can be left to nature, providing you keep the dog out of extremely cold air and drafts until he's completely dry. An easier and better way to dry the dog, especially the furnishings, is to use an electric hair dryer set on low or medium. This method produces fluffier looking furnishings and a nicer appearance to the finished job.

One last note: If your dog gets paint or tar-type substances on his coat, apply a liberal amount of mineral oil to the substance. Let the oil soak in for ten minutes and then rub briskly with an absorbent cloth. Follow with a good bath. Stronger chemicals used to remove paint can cause burning and irritation to the skin that may require subsequent veterinary attention and great suffering to the dog.

Clipping and Scissoring

Clipping a Miniature Schnauzer requires good quality electric clippers. I use an Oster Detachable Blade #A5 clipper with #10 and #15 blades. An Oster #A2 is virtually the same clipper except that the blades must be screwed into place rather than simply snapping in as with the A5. The cost for both is very similar, about $100.00.

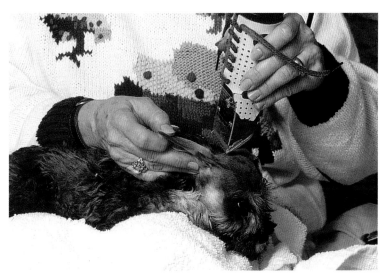

Electric clippers can do a superb grooming job in a short time.

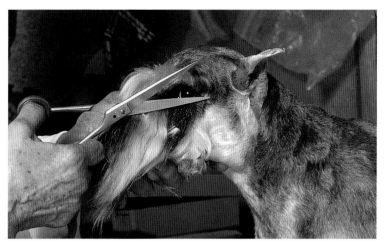

The eyebrows and beard of your Mini Schnauzer must be scissored and proportioned to balance each other, while the cheeks, throat, and front of chest are clipped short.

The process starts with a thorough brushing to remove tangles and debris. Always clip the dog before bathing, never after.

With the clippers running and fitted with a #10 blade and the dog on the table, begin clipping the body at the top of the head following the natural lay of the hair. The body is always clipped from the head toward the tail. Clipping the coat against the natural lay of the hair will cut the hair too short and cause razor burn. Razor burn is painful and can cause open sores. As the sores heal, the dog begins to scratch which, in turn, produces infection that will ultimately require medical attention.

A #15 blade clips under the belly, around the rear, on the ears and throat. Since the #15 blade cuts closer than a #10, care must be taken to assure that you do not injure the skin in these areas.

The hair on the front of the dog is clipped down to his elbows and on the back legs down to his knees (stifle). Hair in the front of the back legs will be blended into the body coat by scissoring.

The overall effect you're looking for when clipping is that of a square dog. When seen in profile, the shape under the chin and head forms a fishhook with a straight line falling down to his front feet.

Eyebrows and beard must be scissored and proportioned to balance each other, while the cheeks, throat, and front of the chest are clipped short.

A well-groomed Miniature Schnauzer indicates a healthy dog with an owner who cares about his pet's welfare and happiness.

Ears should be clipped short as well on both the inside and outside. Then the excess hair inside the ear must be removed with tweezers.

A good groomer knows that the particular cut of the eyebrows and beard is what creates that distinguished Schnauzer look. He or she is also familiar with the Standard of Perfection and knows how to achieve that distinctive terrier expression. That's why it takes so much practice to learn how to properly groom a Miniature Schnauzer. It's also why most owners choose the middle-of-the-road approach to grooming. They want a Miniature Schnauzer that always looks well groomed, so they defer to the professional for the major part of grooming while maintaining the look between groomings.

OTHER GROOMING MATTERS

Finally, let's address the matter of nails and teeth. Tooth and gum care is essential for a healthy mouth. Your veterinarian can teach you how to clean your dog's teeth. He'll suggest the best products for tooth and gum hygiene.

Toenails must be trimmed regularly. If you begin trimming toenails when the puppy is young and teach him to sit still for trimming, you'll have no problem when he becomes an adult. Your vet will teach you how to do this during one of your early visits.

Waiting, however, until the dog is full grown and having him hate nail trimming can be dangerous. By then the dog may attempt to bite the trimmer. This is unacceptable behavior. At this point, the veterinarian will have to muzzle the dog for trimming and you'll have to pay extra for it. So make it economical for yourself and easy on the dog: Teach nail trimming from an early age.

Having a well-groomed Miniature Schnauzer usually indicates a healthy dog and a caring owner who takes great pride in his friend.

HOUSEBREAKING and Training Your Miniature Schnauzer

A few general remarks here seem in order before we get into the individual steps of housebreaking. First of all, Miniature Schnauzers are very easy to housebreak, usually getting the idea of where they are to eliminate within a matter of several days. Some seem to know even before they leave their littermates! Most people teach their dogs to relieve themselves outdoors. Some want or need the relief process to take place indoors. Elderly people who are afraid to go out in inclement weather or after dark, city apartment dwellers who fear the streets late at night, and people of all ages who have unpredictable work schedules may wish their dog to eliminate indoors.

I train all my dogs, regardless of size, to relieve themselves outdoors even in bad weather. Picking up stool from the lawn or curb does not bother me, but patrolling the laundry room for dirty newspapers is just too unpleasant!

Success that comes from luck is usually a happenstance and frequently short lived. Success that comes from well-thought-out, proven methods is often more easily achieved and permanent. The following "Success Method" is designed to give you, the puppy owner, a simple yet proven way to help your puppy develop clean living habits and a feeling of security in his new environment.

If you take your Mini Schnauzer to the same place to eliminate every time, he will soon know what is expected of him.

Most Miniature Schnauzers live as family pets and must conform to the rules of the household. This Schnauzer enjoys the comforts of home.

How to House and Crate Train Your Puppy

Types of Training

Your can train a puppy to relieve himself wherever you choose. For example, city dwellers often train their puppies to relieve themselves in the gutter because large plots of grass are not readily available. Suburbanites, on the other hand, usually have yards to accommodate their dog's needs.

Outdoor training includes such surfaces as grass, dirt, and cement. Indoor training usually means training a dog to newspaper or a paper-lined litter pan (appropriate for small and toy breeds).

When deciding on the surface and location that you'll want your dog to use, be sure it's going to be permanent. Training a dog to grass and then changing your mind two months later is extremely difficult for dog and owner.

Next, choose the command you'll use each and every time you want your puppy to void. "Go hurry up" and "Go make" are examples of commands commonly used by dog owners. Get in the habit of asking the puppy, "Do you want to go hurry up?" (or whatever your chosen relief command is) before you take him out. That way, when he becomes an adult, you'll be able to determine if he wants to

This Mini Schnauzer is not necessarily "in the doghouse" with his master. Even good little puppies need a safe haven to call their own.

go out when you ask him. A confirmation will be signs of interest, wag-ging his tail, watching you intently, going to the door, etc.

Most of all, be consistent. Always take your dog to the same location, always use the same command, and always have him on lead when he's in his relief area.

Offer your puppy clearly defined areas outside in which to eliminate and put him on a schedule to keep him regulated.

By following the Success Method, your puppy will be completely housetrained by the time his muscle and brain development reach maturity. Keep in mind that small breeds usually mature faster than large breeds, but all puppies should be trained by six months of age.

The Puppy's Needs

A puppy needs to relieve himself after play periods, after each meal, after sleeping, and any time he indicates he's looking for a place to urinate or defecate.

The urinary and intestinal tract muscles of very young puppies are not fully developed. Therefore, like human babies, puppies need to relieve themselves frequently.

Take your puppy out often: Every hour for an eight-week-old, for example. The older the puppy, the less often he'll need to relieve himself. Finally, as a mature healthy adult, he'll require only three to five relief trips per day.

Housing

Because the type of housing and control you provide for your puppy has a direct relationship with the success of housetraining, we consider the various aspects of both before we begin training.

Bringing a new puppy home and turning him loose in your house can be compared to turning a child loose in a sports arena and telling the child the place is all his! The sheer enormity of the place would be too much for him to handle.

Instead, offer the puppy clearly defined areas where he can play, sleep, eat, and live. A room of the house where the family gathers the most is the obvious choice. Puppies are social animals and need to feel a part of the pack right from the start. Hearing your voice, watching you while you're doing things, and smelling you nearby are all positive reinforcements that indicate that he is now a member of your pack. Usually a family room, the kitchen, or a nearby adjoining breakfast nook is ideal for providing safety and security for both puppy and owner.

Within that room, there should be a smaller area that the puppy can call his own. A cubby hole, a wire or fiberglass dog crate, or a fenced (not boarded!) corner from which he can view the activities of his new family will be fine.

The size of the area or crate is the key factor here. The area must be large enough for the puppy to lay down and stretch out, as well as stand up without rubbing his head on the top, yet small enough so that he cannot relieve himself at one end and sleep at the other without coming into contact with his droppings.

Dogs are, by nature, clean animals and will not remain close to their relief areas unless forced to do so. In those cases, they then become dirty dogs and usually remain that way for life.

By providing sleeping and resting quarters that fit the dog and offering frequent opportunities to relieve himself outside his quarters, the puppy quickly learns that the outdoors (or the newspaper if you're training him to paper) is the place to go when he needs to urinate or defecate. It also reinforces his innate desire to keep his sleeping quarters clean. This, in turn, helps develop the control muscles that will eventually produce a dog with clean living habits.

The crate or cubby should be lined with a clean towel and the puppy should be offered one toy, no more. Do not put food or water in the crate, as eating and drinking will activate his digestive processes and ultimately defeat your purposes, as well as make the puppy very uncomfortable as he attempts to "hold it."

Never line his sleeping area with newspaper. Puppy litters are usually raised on newspaper and once in your home, the puppy will immediately associate newspaper with voiding. Never put newspaper on any floor while housetraining as this will only confuse the puppy. If you're paper training him, use paper in his designated relief area *only*. Finally, restrict water intake after evening meals. Offer a few licks at a time—never let a young puppy gulp water after meals.

Control

By control we mean helping the puppy to create a lifestyle pattern that will be compatible to that of his human pack. Just as we guide little children to learn our way of life, we must show the puppy when it's time to play, eat, sleep, exercise, even entertain himself.

Your puppy should always sleep in his crate. He should also learn that during times of household confusion and excessive human activity, such as a breakfast when family members are preparing for the day, he can play by himself in relative safety and comfort in his crate. Each time you leave the puppy alone, he should be crated. Puppies are chewers. They can't tell the difference between lamp cords, television wires, shoes, or table legs. Chewing into a television wire, for example, can be fatal to the puppy, while a shorted wire can start a fire in the house.

If the puppy chews on the arm of a chair when he's alone, you will probably discipline him angrily when you get home. Thus he makes the association that your coming home means he's going to

Puppies have short attentions spans, so when training your young Mini Schnauzer, remember to keep the lessons short and to make it fun for both you and your dog.

be hit or punished. (He won't remember chewing up the chair and is incapable of making the association of the discipline with his naughty deed.)

If you have a small child in the home that wants to get into the puppy's food bowl every time he eats, feeding the pup in his crate is the answer. The child can't disturb the dog, and the pup will be free to eat in peace.

Other times of excitement, such as family parties, can be fun for the puppy providing he can view the activities from the security of his crate. He's not underfoot, he's not being fed all sorts of tidbits that will probably cause him stomach distress, yet he still feels part of the fun.

Schedule

As stated earlier, a puppy should be taken to his relief area each time he's released from his crate, after meals, after a play session, when he first awakens in the morning (at eight weeks of age, this can mean five in the morning!) and whenever he indicates by circling or sniffing that he needs to urinate or defecate. For puppies under 10 weeks of age, a routine of taking him out every hour is necessary. As the puppy grows, he'll be able to wait for longer periods of time.

The Miniature Schnauzer that is given plenty of opportunity to exercise is a happier and healthier companion. These two friends take a stroll together.

Keep trips to his relief area short. Stay no more than five to six minutes and then return to the house. If he goes during that time, praise lavishly and take him indoors immediately. If he doesn't, but he has an accident when you go back indoors, pick him up immediately, say "No! No!" and return to his relief area. Wait a few minutes, then return to the house again. *Never* hit a puppy or rub his face in urine or excrement when he has had an accident!

Once indoors, put him in his crate until you've had time to clean up his accident. Then

Seventeen-week-old Maggie, owned by Norma Steill and Marge Ditz, waits patiently for a treat.

release him to the family area and watch him more closely than before. Chances are, his accident was a result of your not picking up his signal or waiting too long before offering him the opportunity to relieve himself. *Never* hold a grudge against the puppy for accidents.

The puppy should also have regular play and exercise sessions when he's with you or a family member. Exercise for a very young puppy can consist of a short walk around the house or yard. Playing can include fetching games with a large ball or an old sock with a knot tied in the middle. (All puppies teethe and need soft things on which to chew.) Remember to restrict play periods to indoors within his living area (the family room, for example) until he's completely house trained.

Let the puppy learn that going outdoors means it's time to relieve himself, not play. Once trained, he'll be able to play indoors and out and still differentiate the times for play versus the times for relief.

Help him develop regular hours for naps, being alone, playing by himself, and just resting, all in his crate. Encourage him to entertain himself while you're busy with your activities. Let him learn that having you near is comforting, but your main purpose in life is not to provide him with undivided attention.

Each time you put the puppy in his crate, tell him, "It's cubby time!" (or whatever command you choose). Soon, he'll run to his crate when he hears you say those words.

In the beginning of his training, don't leave him in his crate for prolonged periods of time, except during the night when everyone is sleeping. Make his experience with his crate a pleasant one and, as an adult, he'll love it and willingly stay in it for several hours. (There are millions of people who go to work every day and leave their adult dogs crated while they're away. The dogs accept this as their lifestyle and look forward to "crate time.")

Crate training provides safety for you, the puppy, and the home. It also provides the puppy with a feeling of security that helps develop a puppy with self confidence and clean habits.

When crate training your dog, provide him with a variety of toys to keep him occupied.

It's okay to allow your dog freedom to roam around the house when you are home, but for his own safety, put him in his crate or a partitioned-off room when you must leave him.

SIX STEPS TO SUCCESSFUL CRATE TRAINING

Remember, one of the primary ingredients in house training your puppy is control. Regardless of your lifestyle, there will always be occasions when you'll need to have a place where your dog can stay and be happy and safe. Crate training is the answer for now and in the future.

Below are the step-by-step directions to actually training your puppy to accept his crate as his den, a place of security and comfort. Follow each step in order and don't try to rush the final steps. A conscientious approach to training now will result in a happy dog that willingly accepts your lifestyle as his own.

1. Tell the puppy, "It's cubby time!" and place him in the crate with a small treat (a piece of cheese or half a biscuit). Let him stay in the crate for five minutes while you are in the same room. Then release him and praise lavishly. Never release him when he's fussing. Wait until he's quiet before you let him out.

2. Repeat Step 1 several times a day.

3. The next day, place the puppy in the crate as before. Let him stay there for ten minutes. Do this several times.

4. Continue building time in five minute increments until the puppy will stay in his crate for 30 minutes with you in the room. Always take him to his relief area after prolonged periods in his crate.

5. Now go back to the beginning and let the puppy stay in his crate for five minutes while you are out of the room.

6. Once again build crate time in five minute increments with you out of the room. When puppy will stay willingly in his crate (he may even fall asleep!) for 30 minutes with you out of the room, he'll be ready to stay in it for several hours at a time.

Conclusion

A few key elements are really all you need to a successful house and crate training method—consistency, frequency, praise, control, and supervision. By following these procedures with a normal healthy puppy, you and the puppy will soon be past the stage of "accidents" and ready to move on to a full rewarding life together.

In addition to his crate, you may want to provide your Miniature Schnauzer puppy with a soft bed he can use at will whenever he's

With persistence, patience, and praise, your Mini Schnauzer puppy can learn any command you wish to teach him. This pup practices his sit.

Once your dog is housetrained you can begin training him to obey commands and participate in dog sports such as agility.

in the house but not in his crate. A bean bag bed or covered foam bed is ideal for this purpose. Oval wicker baskets are nice, but offer too much opportunity for destructive chewing. Even foam sides that may be at the level of the dog's mouth can be just too tempting to chew upon. Bean bag beds are best because the centers are depressed yet the sides don't easily lend themselves to those sharp little puppy teeth.

When he's in his soft bed you must supervise him and take the bed away if he decides to use it as a chew toy. Waiting until he's completed the teething process will ensure that he doesn't develop bad habits of chewing on furniture.

Speaking of furniture, it's wise to decide before you bring your new puppy home whether or not you intend to allow him on your furniture. Remember that if you allow him on the furniture as a puppy, you'll have to do it when he's an adult.

Miniature Schnauzers don't shed hair onto furniture or clothes, so most owners do allow their dogs on their furniture. However, if you have any reservations about this, set your rules now and stick to them. The puppy can and will adjust to your wishes providing you let him know what you do and do not want and you remain consistent in your decisions.

If you decide that the furniture should be reserved for people, then teach him that sofas, chairs, and human beds are off-limits. When he attempts to jump up onto a piece of furniture, say "No, off!" in a stern voice and remove him immediately. If he looks at you and turns away, tell him he's a "Good boy!"

If he persists in jumping on a particular piece of furniture, gather a collection of hard objects such as pots and pans, telephone books, and canned goods and literally cover the seat with the objects. Say nothing to the dog and set up this little trap while he's out of sight.

The next time the puppy goes to jump onto the furniture, he'll be faced with an array of clanging and uncomfortable items that prohibit him from making himself at home. Chances are he'll jump off to the comfort and safety of the floor, at which point you can tell him what a good boy he is.

Don't recognize his attempt to get on the furniture, but do recognize his being on the floor. Remember that recognizing positive behavior and ignoring negative behavior is a lot more successful when developing desirable habits.

Puppy classes are a great way to teach your Mini Schnauzer basic obedience and build confidence. Maggie and owner Marge Ditz learn to negotiate the cat walk.

Finally, let's talk about training your Miniature Schnauzer. If you recall our earlier discussion of Miniature Schnauzer characteristics, you'll remember reading that he is a multitalented dog genetically engineered to be successful at many things. As such they should never be allowed to vegetate or become couch potatoes.

The subsequent boredom that doing nothing produces can easily cause them to get into all manner of mischief. Instead, put those bright minds and capable bodies to work—let them be useful members of your pack, teach them tricks, give them the opportunity to participate in sporting activities, in order words—do something!

You'll want to begin your Miniature Schnauzer's training by enrolling him in a puppy class. Kindergarten classes are for puppies from 8 to 20 weeks of age and teach the puppy good manners, as well as what is and is not acceptable behavior, and they reinforce that you are the pack leader.

Beginner's obedience classes are for puppies from five months and over. The lessons are similar, and both classes, when taught by knowledgeable and caring instructors, help you and your puppy build a bond together that will last a lifetime. Your puppy will learn to sit, stand, down, come, and stay on command. He'll learn to accept other dogs and people with gentleness and respect. He'll learn not to jump on people and to sit quietly for attention when your friends wish to greet him.

Miniature Schnauzers do not respond well to rough training methods. They're bright and need only to be shown a few times what you want them to do and they always appear to be so proud of themselves when you show your appreciation of their compliance.

When searching for a good training facility, be sure the school has a reputation of humane and gentle training methods. Ask your veterinarian, friends, and other dog owners for references. Observe a class in session if you can evaluate what you see. Are the dogs happy? Do the owners and dogs work well together? Are the teachers friendly and helpful?

When you've completed your Miniature Schnauzer's basic training, he'll be ready to discover some of the activities in my book. Try teaching him some tricks and how to be a home helper, for starters. As you and your dog become experienced at learning together, you'll discover a wondrous world out there that will add meaning to every day for the rest of your lives together. That's what Miniature Schnauzers do!

SPORT of Purebred Dogs

Welcome to the exciting and sometimes frustrating sport of dogs. No doubt you are trying to learn more about dogs or you wouldn't be deep into this book. This section covers the basics that may entice you, further your knowledge and help you to understand the dog world.

Dog showing has been a very popular sport for a long time and has been taken quite seriously by some. Others only enjoy it as a hobby.

The Kennel Club in England was formed in 1859, the American Kennel Club was established in 1884 and the Canadian Kennel Club was formed in 1888. The purpose of these clubs was to register purebred dogs and maintain their Stud Books. In the beginning, the concept of registering dogs was not readily accepted. More than 36 million dogs have been enrolled in the AKC Stud Book since its inception in 1888. Presently the kennel clubs not only register dogs but adopt and enforce rules and regulations governing dog shows, obedience trials and field trials. Over the years they have fostered and encouraged interest in the health and welfare of the purebred dog. They routinely donate funds to veterinary research for study on genetic disorders.

Below are the addresses of the kennel clubs in the United States, Great Britain and Canada.

The American Kennel Club
260 Madison Avenue
New York, NY 10016
or 5580 Centerview Drive,
Raleigh, NC 27606

The Kennel Club
1 Clarges Street
Picadilly, London, WIY 8AB, England

The Canadian Kennel Club
89 Skyway Avenue
Suite 100
Etobicoke, Ontario, Canada M9W 6R4

Today there are numerous activities that are enjoyable for both the dog and the handler. Some of the activities include conformation showing, obedience competition, tracking, agility, the Canine Good Citizen Certificate, and a wide range of instinct tests that vary from breed to breed. Where you start depends upon your goals which early on may not be readily apparent.

Puppy Kindergarten

Every puppy will benefit from this class. PKT is the foundation for all future dog activities from conformation to "couch potatoes." Pet owners should make an effort to attend even if they never expect to show their dog. The class is designed for puppies about three months of age with graduation at approximately five months of age. All the puppies will be in the same age group and, even though some may be a little unruly, there should not be any real problem. This

With the proper training, your Miniature Schnauzer can excel in any activity. Bee's BB Gunn, owned by Beatrice Smith, shows off the fruits of her labor.

class will teach the puppy some beginning obedience. As in all obedience classes the owner learns how to train his own dog. The PKT class gives the puppy the opportunity to interact with other puppies in the same age group and exposes him to strangers, which is very important. Some dogs grow up with behavior problems, one of them being fear of strangers. As you can see, there can be much to gain from this class.

There are some basic obedience exercises that every dog should learn. Some of these can be started with puppy kindergarten.

Sit

One way of teaching the sit is to have your dog on your left side with the leash in your right hand, close to the collar. Pull up on the leash and at the same time reach around his hindlegs with your left hand and tuck them in. As you are doing this say, "Beau, sit." Always use the dog's name when you give an active command. Some owners like to use a treat holding it over the dog's head. The dog will need to sit to get the treat. Encourage the dog to hold the sit for a few seconds, which will eventually be the beginning of the Sit/Stay. Depending on how cooperative he is, you can rub him under the chin or stroke his back. It is a good time to establish eye contact.

Down

Sit the dog on your left side and kneel down beside him with the leash in your right hand. Reach over him with your left hand and

Hand signals in conjunction with verbal commands can be very effective. This Mini Schnauzer practices the down command.

Keen and enthusiastic, the Miniature Schnauzer takes to obedience work easily. Maxwell and owner Dot Robbins participate in an obedience competition.

grasp his left foreleg. With your right hand, take his right foreleg and pull his legs forward while you say, "Beau, down." If he tries to get up, lean on his shoulder to encourage him to stay down. It will relax your dog if you stroke his back while he is down. Try to encourage him to stay down for a few seconds as preparation for the Down/Stay.

Heel

The definition of heeling is the dog walking under control at your left heel. Your puppy will learn controlled walking in the puppy kindergarten class, which will eventually lead to heeling. The command is "Beau, heel," and you start off briskly with your left foot. Your leash is in your right hand and your left hand is holding it about half way down. Your left hand should be able to control the leash and there should be a little slack in it. You want him to walk with you with your leg somewhere between his nose and his shoulder. You need to encourage him to stay with you, not forging (in front of you) or lagging behind you. It is best to keep him on a fairly short lead. Do not allow the lead to become tight. It is far better to give him a little jerk when necessary and remind him to heel. When you come to a halt, be prepared physically to make him sit. It takes practice to become coordinated. There are excellent books on training that you may wish to purchase. Your instructor should be able to recommend one for you.

Recall

This quite possibly is the most important exercise you will ever teach. It should be a pleasant experience. The puppy may learn to do random recalls while being attached to a long line such as a clothes line. Later the exercise will start with the dog sitting and staying until called. The command is "Beau, come." Let your command be happy. You want your dog to come willingly and faithfully. The recall could save his life if he sneaks out the door. In practicing the recall, let him jump on you or touch you before you reach for him. If he is shy, then kneel down to his level. Reaching for the insecure dog could frighten him, and he may not be willing to come again in the future. Lots of praise and a treat would be in order whenever you do a recall. Under no circumstances should you ever correct your dog when he has come to you. Later in formal obedience your dog will be required to sit in front of you after recalling and then go to heel position.

CONFORMATION

Conformation showing is our oldest dog show sport. This type of showing is based on the dog's appearance—that is his structure, movement and attitude. When considering this type of showing, you need to be aware of your breed's standard and be able to evaluate your dog compared to that standard. The breeder of your puppy or other experienced breeders would be good sources for such an evaluation. Puppies can go through lots of changes over a period of time. Many puppies start out as promising hopefuls and then after maturing may be disappointing as show candidates. Even so this should not deter them from being excellent pets.

Usually conformation training classes are offered by the local kennel or obedience clubs. These are excellent places for training puppies. The puppy should be able to walk on a lead before entering such a class. Proper ring procedure and technique for posing (stacking) the dog will be demonstrated as well as gaiting the dog. Usually certain patterns are used in the ring such as the triangle or the "L." Conformation class, like the PKT class, will give your youngster the opportunity to socialize with different breeds of dogs and humans too.

Successful showing takes dedication and preparation but most of all, it should be an enjoyable experience for both owners and dogs alike.

It takes some time to learn the routine of conformation showing. Usually one starts at the puppy matches that may be AKC Sanctioned or Fun Matches. These matches are generally for puppies from two or three months to a year old, and there may be classes for the adult over the age of 12 months. Similar to point shows, the classes are divided by sex and after completion of the classes in that breed or variety, the class winners compete for Best of Breed or Variety. The winner goes on to compete in the Group and the Group winners compete for Best in Match. No championship points are awarded for match wins.

A few matches can be great training for puppies even though there is no intention to go on showing. Matches enable the puppy to meet new people and be handled by a stranger—the judge. It is also a change of environment, which broadens the horizon for both dog and handler. Matches and other dog activities boost the confidence of the handler and especially the younger handlers.

Earning an AKC championship is built on a point system, which is different from Great Britain. To become an AKC Champion of Record the dog must earn 15 points. The number of points earned each time depends upon the number of dogs in competition. The number of points available at each show depends upon the breed, its sex and the location of the show. The United States is divided into ten AKC zones. Each zone has its own set of points. The purpose of the zones is to try to equalize the points available from breed to breed and area to area. The AKC adjusts the point scale annually.

The number of points that can be won at a show are between one and five. Three-, four- and five-point wins are considered majors. Not only does the dog need 15 points won under three different judges, but those points must include two majors under two different judges. Canada also works on a point system but majors are not required.

Dogs always show before bitches. The classes available to those seeking points are: Puppy (which may be divided into 6 to 9 months and 9 to 12 months); 12 to 18 months; Novice; Bred-by-Exhibitor; American-bred; and Open. The class winners of the same sex of each breed or variety compete against each other for Winners Dog and Winners Bitch. A Reserve Winners Dog and Reserve Winners Bitch are also awarded but do not carry any points unless the Winners win is disallowed by AKC. The Winners Dog and Bitch compete with the specials (those dogs that have attained championship) for Best of Breed or Variety, Best of Winners and Best of Opposite Sex. It is possible to pick up an extra point or even a major if the points are higher for the defeated winner than those of Best of Winners. The latter would get the higher total from the defeated winner.

At an all-breed show, each Best of Breed or Variety winner will go on to his respective Group and then the Group winners will compete against each other for Best in Show. There are seven

People love a parade—and so do Mini Schnauzers! Maxwell and Dot Robbins perform with the Hot Springs National Park Kennel Club.

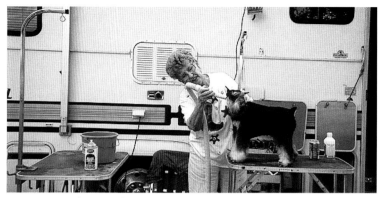

A Miniature Schnauzer that competes in the show ring must become accustomed to extensive grooming procedures.

Groups: Sporting, Hounds, Working, Terriers, Toys, Non-Sporting and Herding. Obviously there are no Groups at speciality shows (those shows that have only one breed or a show such as the American Spaniel Club's Flushing Spaniel Show, which is for all flushing spaniel breeds).

Earning a championship in England is somewhat different since they do not have a point system. Challenge Certificates are awarded if the judge feels the dog is deserving regardless of the number of dogs in competition. A dog must earn three Challenge Certificates under three different judges, with at least one of these Certificates being won after the age of 12 months. Competition is very strong and entries may be higher than they are in the U.S. The Kennel Club's Challenge Certificates are only available at Championship Shows.

In England, The Kennel Club regulations require that certain dogs, Border Collies and Gundog breeds, qualify in a working capacity (i.e., obedience or field trials) before becoming a full Champion. If they do not qualify in the working aspect, then they are designated a Show Champion, which is equivalent to the AKC's Champion of Record. A Gundog may be granted the title of Field Trial Champion (FT Ch.) if it passes all the tests in the field but would also have to qualify in conformation before becoming a full Champion. A Border Collie that earns the title of Obedience Champion (Ob Ch.) must also qualify in the conformation ring before becoming a Champion.

The U.S. doesn't have a designation full Champion but does award for Dual and Triple Champions. The Dual Champion must be a Champion of Record, and either Champion Tracker, Herding Champion, Obedience Trial Champion or Field Champion. Any dog that has been awarded the titles of Champion of Record, and any two of the following: Champion Tracker, Herding Champion, Obedience Trial Champion or Field Champion, may be designated as a Triple Champion.

The shows in England seem to put more emphasis on breeder judges than those in the U.S. There is much competition within the breeds. Therefore the quality of the individual breeds should be very good. In the United States we tend to have more "all around judges" (those that judge multiple breeds) and use the breeder judges at the specialty shows. Breeder judges are more familiar with their own breed since they are actively breeding that breed or did so at one time. Americans emphasize Group and Best in Show wins and promote them accordingly.

The shows in England can be very large and extend over several days, with the Groups being scheduled on different days. Though multi-day shows are not common in the U.S., there are cluster shows, where several different clubs will use the same show site over consecutive days.

Westminster Kennel Club is our most prestigious show although the entry is limited to 2500. In recent years, entry has been limited to Champions. This show is more formal than the majority of the shows with the judges wearing formal attire and the handlers fashionably dressed. In most instances the quality of the dogs is superb. After all, it is a show of Champions. It is a good show to study the AKC registered breeds and is by far the most exciting— especially since it is televised! WKC is one of the few shows in this country that is still benched. This means the dog must be in his benched area during the show hours except when he is being groomed, in the ring, or being exercised.

Typically, the handlers are very particular about their appearances. They are careful not to wear something that will detract from their dog but will perhaps enhance it. American ring procedure is quite formal compared to that of other countries. There is a certain etiquette expected between the judge and exhibitor and among the other exhibitors. Of course it is not always the case but the judge is supposed to be polite, not engaging in small talk or acknowledging how well he knows the handler. There is a more informal and relaxed atmosphere at the shows in other countries. For instance,

Training allows the Miniature Schnauzer and his owner to develop a closeness formed from working together.

the dress code is more casual. I can see where this might be more fun for the exhibitor and especially for the novice. The U.S. is very handler-oriented in many of the breeds. It is true, in most instances, that the experienced professional handler can present the dog better and will have a feel for what a judge likes.

In England, Crufts is The Kennel Club's own show and is most assuredly the largest dog show in the world. They've been known to have an entry of nearly 20,000, and the show lasts four days. Entry is only gained by qualifying through winning in specified classes at another Championship Show. Westminster is strictly conformation, but Crufts exhibitors and spectators enjoy not only conformation but obedience, agility and a multitude of exhibitions as well. Obedience was admitted in 1957 and agility in 1983.

If you are handling your own dog, please give some consideration to your apparel. For sure the dress code at matches is more informal than the point shows. However, you should wear something a little more appropriate than beach attire or ragged jeans and bare feet. If you check out the handlers and see what is presently fashionable, you'll catch on. Men usually dress with a shirt and tie and a nice sports coat. Whether you are male or female, you will want to wear comfortable clothes and shoes. You need to be able to run with your dog and you certainly don't want to take a chance of falling and hurting yourself. Heaven forbid, if nothing else, you'll upset your dog. Women usually wear a dress or two-piece outfit, preferably with pockets to carry bait, comb, brush, etc. In this case men are the lucky ones with all their pockets. Ladies, think about where your dress will be if you need to kneel on

In conformation, your Mini Schnauzer will be evaluated on how closely he conforms to the breed standard.

An exercise pen is just one of the many pieces of equipment you will need to bring with you to a dog show.

the floor and also think about running. Does it allow freedom to do so?

You need to take along dog; crate; ex pen (if you use one); extra newspaper; water pail and water; all required grooming equipment, including hair dryer and extension cord; table; chair for you; bait for dog and lunch for you and friends; and, last but not least, clean up materials, such as plastic bags, paper towels, and perhaps a bath towel and some shampoo—just in case. Don't forget your entry confirmation and directions to the show.

If you are showing in obedience, then you will want to wear pants. Many of our top obedience handlers wear pants that are color-coordinated with their dogs. The philosophy is that imperfections in the black dog will be less obvious next to your black pants.

Whether you are showing in conformation, Junior Showmanship or obedience, you need to watch the clock and be sure you are not late. It is customary to pick up your conformation armband a few minutes before the start of the class. They will not wait for you and if you are on the show grounds and not in the ring, you will upset everyone. It's a little more complicated picking up your obedience armband if you show later in the class. If you have not picked up your armband and they get to your number, you may not be allowed to show. It's best to pick up your armband early, but then you may show earlier than expected if other handlers don't pick up. Customarily all conflicts should be discussed with the judge prior to the start of the class.

Junior Showmanship

The Junior Showmanship Class is a wonderful way to build self confidence even if there are no aspirations of staying with the dog-show game later in life. Frequently, Junior Showmanship becomes the background of those who become successful exhibitors/handlers in the future. In some instances it is taken very seriously, and success is measured in terms of wins. The Junior Handler is judged solely on his ability and skill in presenting his dog. The dog's conformation is not to be considered by the judge. Even so the condition and grooming of the dog may be a reflection upon the handler.

Usually the matches and point shows include different classes. The Junior Handler's dog may be entered in a breed or obedience class and even shown by another person in that class. Junior Showmanship classes are usually divided by age and perhaps sex. The age is determined by the handler's age on the day of the show. The classes are:

CANINE GOOD CITIZEN®

The AKC sponsors a program to encourage dog owners to train their dogs. Local clubs perform the pass/fail tests, and dogs who pass are awarded a Canine Good Citizen® Certificate. Proof of vaccination is required at the time of participation. The test includes:
1. Accepting a friendly stranger.
2. Sitting politely for petting.
3. Appearance and grooming.
4. Walking on a loose leash.
5. Walking through a crowd.
6. Sit and down on command/staying in place.
7. Come when called.
8. Reaction to another dog.

9. Reactions to distractions.
10. Supervised separation.

If more effort was made by pet owners to accomplish these exercises, fewer dogs would be cast off to the humane shelter.

OBEDIENCE

Obedience is necessary, without a doubt, but it can also become a wonderful hobby or even an obsession. Obedience classes and competition can provide wonderful companionship, not only with your dog but with your classmates or fellow competitors. It is always gratifying to discuss your dog's problems with others who have had similar experiences. The AKC acknowledged Obedience around 1936, and it has changed tremendously even though many of the exercises are basically the same. Today, obedience competition is just that—very competitive. Even so, it is possible for every obedience exhibitor to come home a winner (by earning qualifying scores) even though he/she may not earn a placement in the class.

There are many activities in which the versatile and intelligent Mini Schnauzer can compete. Bee's BB Gunn demonstrates his talent in scent discrimination.

Most of the obedience titles are awarded after earning three qualifying scores (legs) in the appropriate class under three different judges. These classes offer a perfect score of 200, which is extremely rare. Each of the class exercises has its own point value. A leg is earned after receiving a score of at least 170 and at least 50 percent of the points available in each exercise. The titles are:

Companion Dog—CD
Companion Dog Excellent—CDX
Utility Dog—UD

After achieving the UD title, you may feel inclined to go after the UDX and/or OTCh. The UDX (Utility Dog Excellent) title went into effect in January 1994. It is not easily attained. The title requires qualifying simultaneously ten times in Open B and Utility B but not necessarily at consecutive shows.

The OTCh (Obedience Trial Champion) is awarded after the dog has earned his UD and then goes on to earn 100 championship points, a first place in Utility, a first place in Open and another first place in either class. The placements must be won under three different judges at all-breed obedience trials. The points are determined by the number of dogs competing in the Open B and Utility B classes. The OTCh title precedes the dog's name.

Obedience competitions are available through local clubs and offer practice and experience for your Mini Schnauzer. Black Jack and owner Dot Robbins compete in a fun match.

Once your Mini Schnauzer masters basic obedience, he can go on to compete in events like agility. Mandy and owner Lynn Baitinger negotiate the teeter totter.

Obedience matches (AKC Sanctioned, Fun, and Show and Go) are usually available. Usually they are sponsored by the local obedience clubs. When preparing an obedience dog for a title, you will find matches very helpful. Fun Matches and Show and Go Matches are more lenient in allowing you to make corrections in the ring. This type of training is usually very necessary for the Open and Utility Classes. AKC Sanctioned Obedience Matches do not allow corrections in the ring since they must abide by the AKC Obedience Regulations. If you are interested in showing in obedience, then you should contact the AKC for a copy of the Obedience Regulations.

TRACKING

Tracking is officially classified obedience. There are three tracking titles available: Tracking Dog (TD), Tracking Dog Excellent (TDX), Variable Surface Tracking (VST). If all three tracking titles are obtained, then the dog officially becomes a CT (Champion Tracker). The CT will go in front of the dog's name.

A TD may be earned anytime and does not have to follow the other obedience titles. There are many exhibitors that prefer tracking to obedience, and there are others who do both.

AGILITY

Agility was first introduced by John Varley in England at the Crufts Dog Show, February 1978, but Peter Meanwell, competitor and judge, actually developed the idea. It was officially recognized in the early '80s. Agility is extremely popular in England and Canada and growing in popularity in the U.S. The AKC acknowledged agility in August 1994. Dogs must be at least 12 months of age to be entered. It is a fascinating sport that the dog, handler and spectators enjoy to the utmost. Agility is a spectator sport! The dog performs off lead. The handler either runs with his dog or positions himself on the course and directs his dog with verbal and hand signals over a timed course over or through a variety of obstacles including a time out or pause. One of the main

Cracker Jack Surprise, UD, owned by Kristy Lockhard, conquers the broad jump at an obedience trial.

Agility is an action-packed sport that is thrilling for both the dogs and spectators alike.

drawbacks to agility is finding a place to train. The obstacles take up a lot of space and it is very time consuming to put up and take down courses.

The titles earned at AKC agility trials are Novice Agility Dog (NAD), Open Agility Dog (OAD), Agility Dog Excellent (ADX), and Master Agility Excellent (MAX). In order to acquire an agility title, a dog must earn a qualifying score in its respective class on three separate occasions under two different judges. The MAX will be awarded after earning ten qualifying scores in the Agility Excellent Class.

PERFORMANCE TESTS

During the last decade the American Kennel Club has promoted performance tests—those events that test the different breeds' natural abilities. This type of event encourages a handler to devote even more time to his dog and retain the natural instincts of his breed heritage. It is an important part of the wonderful world of dogs.

Training to compete is not an easy task, but the satisfaction you'll receive when you accomplish your goals is truly rewarding.

General Information

Obedience, tracking and agility allow the purebred dog with an Indefinite Listing Privilege (ILP) number or a limited registration to be exhibited and earn titles. Application must be made to the AKC for an ILP number.

The American Kennel Club publishes a monthly *Events* magazine that is part of the *Gazette*, their official journal for the sport of purebred dogs. The *Events* section lists upcoming shows and the secretary or superintendent for them. The majority of the conformation shows in the U.S. are overseen by licensed superintendents. Generally the entry closing date is approximately two-and-a-half weeks before the actual show. Point shows are fairly expensive, while the match shows cost about one third of the point show entry fee. Match shows usually take entries the day of the show but some are pre-entry. The best way to find match show information is through your local kennel club. Upon asking, the AKC can provide you with a list of superintendents, and you can write and ask to be put on their mailing lists.

Obedience trial and tracking test information is available through the AKC. Frequently these events are not superintended, but put on by the host club. Therefore you would make the entry with the event's secretary.

As you have read, there are numerous activities you can share with your dog. Regardless what you do, it does take teamwork. Your dog can only benefit from your attention and training. We hope this chapter has enlightened you and hope, if nothing else, you will attend a show here and there. Perhaps you will start with a puppy kindergarten class, and who knows where it may lead!

HEALTH CARE

Veterinary medicine has become far more sophisticated than what was available to our ancestors. This can be attributed to the increase in household pets and consequently the demand for better care for them. Also human medicine has become far more complex. Today diagnostic testing in veterinary medicine parallels human diagnostics. Because of better technology we can expect our pets to live healthier lives thereby increasing their life spans.

THE FIRST CHECK UP

You will want to take your new puppy/dog in for its first check up within 48 to 72 hours after acquiring it. Many breeders strongly recommend this check up and so do the humane shelters. A puppy/dog can appear healthy but it may have a serious problem that is not apparent to the layman. Most pets have some type of a minor flaw that may never cause a real problem.

Unfortunately if he/she should have a serious problem, you will want to consider the consequences of keeping the pet and the attachments that will be formed, which may be broken prematurely. Keep in mind there are many healthy dogs looking for good homes.

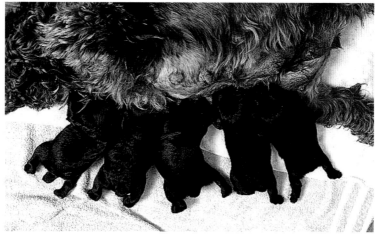

Puppies receive their first immunities from their mother, but will soon need to be vaccinated against certain diseases.

Your new Mini Schnauzer puppy will need to visit the veterinarian within the first 48 hours after you acquire him.

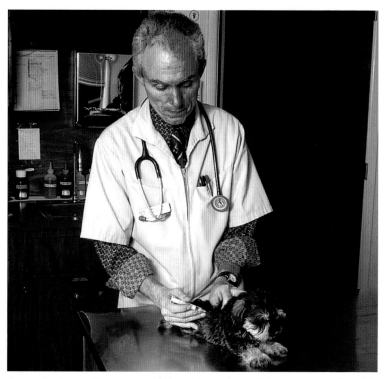

Immunizations will protect your vulnerable Miniature Schnauzer puppy from life-threatening diseases.

This first check up is a good time to establish yourself with the veterinarian and learn the office policy regarding their hours and how they handle emergencies. Usually the breeder or another conscientious pet owner is a good reference for locating a capable veterinarian. You should be aware that not all veterinarians give the same quality of service. Please do not make your selection on the least expensive clinic, as they may be short changing your pet. There is the possibility that eventually it will cost you more due to improper diagnosis, treatment, etc. If you are selecting a new veterinarian, feel free to ask for a tour of the clinic. You should inquire about making an appointment for a tour since all clinics are working clinics, and therefore may not be available all day for sightseers. You may worry less if you see where your pet will be spending the day if he ever needs to be hospitalized.

The Physical Exam

Your veterinarian will check your pet's overall condition, which includes listening to the heart; checking the respiration; feeling the abdomen, muscles and joints; checking the mouth, which includes the gum color and signs of gum disease along with plaque buildup; checking the ears for signs of an infection or ear mites; examining the eyes; and, last but not least, checking the condition of the skin and coat.

He should ask you questions regarding your pet's eating and elimination habits and invite you to relay your questions. It is a good idea to prepare a list so as not to forget anything. He should discuss the proper diet and the quantity to be fed. If this should differ from your breeder's recommendation, then you should convey to him the breeder's choice and see if he approves. If he recommends changing the diet, then this should be done over a few days so as not to cause a gastrointestinal upset. It is customary to take in a fresh stool sample (just a small amount) for a test for intestinal parasites. It must be fresh, preferably within 12 hours, since the eggs hatch quickly and after hatching will not be observed under the microscope. If your pet isn't obliging then, usually the technician can take one in the clinic.

Immunizations

It is important that you take your puppy/dog's vaccination record with you on your first visit. In case of a puppy, presumably

Good preventative health care throughout your dog's life will result in a happier healthier pet.

the breeder has seen to the vaccinations up to the time you acquired custody. Veterinarians differ in their vaccination protocol. It is not unusual for your puppy to have received vaccinations for distemper, hepatitis, leptospirosis, parvovirus and parainfluenza every two to three weeks from the age of five or six weeks. Usually this is a combined injection and is typically called the DHLPP. The DHLPP is given through at least 12 to 14 weeks of age, and it is customary to continue with another parvovirus vaccine at 16 to 18 weeks. You may wonder why so many immunizations are necessary. No one knows for sure when the puppy's maternal antibodies are gone, although it is customarily accepted that distemper antibodies are gone by 12 weeks. Usually parvovirus antibodies are gone by 16 to 18 weeks of age. However, it is possible for the maternal antibodies to be gone at a much earlier age or even a later age. Therefore immunizations are started at an early age. The vaccine will not give immunity as long as there are maternal antibodies.

The rabies vaccination is given at three or six months of age depending on your local laws. A vaccine for bordetella (kennel cough) is advisable and can be given anytime from the age of five weeks. The coronavirus is not commonly given unless there is a problem locally. The Lyme vaccine is necessary in endemic areas. Lyme disease has been reported in 47 states.

Dogs can pick up diseases from other dogs, so make sure your Mini Schnauzer has his proper vaccinations before taking him out to make friends.

Distemper

This is virtually an incurable disease. If the dog recovers, he is subject to severe nervous disorders. The virus attacks every tissue in the body and resembles a bad cold with a fever. It can cause a runny nose and eyes and cause gastrointestinal disorders, including a poor appetite, vomiting and diarrhea. The virus is carried by raccoons, foxes, wolves, mink and other dogs. Unvaccinated youngsters and senior citizens are very susceptible. This is still a common disease.

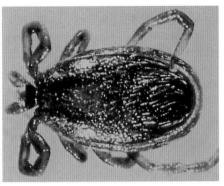

The deer tick is the most common carrier of Lyme disease. Photo courtesy of Virbac Laboratories, Inc., Fort Worth, Texas.

Hepatitis

This is a virus that is most serious in very young dogs. It is spread by contact with an infected animal or its stool or urine. The virus affects the liver and kidneys and is characterized by high fever, depression and lack of appetite. Recovered animals may be afflicted with chronic illnesses.

Leptospirosis

This is a bacterial disease transmitted by contact with the urine of an infected dog, rat or other wildlife. It produces severe symptoms of fever, depression, jaundice and internal bleeding and was fatal before the vaccine was developed. Recovered dogs can be carriers, and the disease can be transmitted from dogs to humans.

Parvovirus

This was first noted in the late 1970s and is still a fatal disease. However, with proper vaccinations, early diagnosis and prompt treatment, it is a manageable disease. It attacks the bone marrow and intestinal tract. The symptoms include depression, loss of appetite, vomiting, diarrhea and collapse. Immediate medical attention is of the essence.

Well-cared-for Mini Schnauzers can enjoy a long and fruitful life. Spring Along Black Poppy, at 13 years of age, would have to agree!

Rabies

This is shed in the saliva and is carried by raccoons, skunks, foxes, other dogs and cats. It attacks nerve tissue, resulting in paralysis and death. Rabies can be transmitted to people and is virtually always fatal. This disease is reappearing in the suburbs.

Bordetella (Kennel Cough)

The symptoms are coughing, sneezing, hacking and retching accompanied by nasal discharge usually lasting from a few days to several weeks. There are several disease-producing organisms responsible for this disease. The present vaccines are helpful but do not protect for all the strains. It usually is not life threatening but in some instances it can progress to a serious bronchopneumonia. The disease is highly contagious. The vaccination should be given routinely for dogs that come in contact with other dogs, such as through boarding, training class or visits to the groomer.

Coronavirus

This is usually self limiting and not life threatening. It was first noted in the late '70s about a year before parvovirus. The virus produces a yellow/brown stool and there may be depression, vomiting and diarrhea.

Lyme Disease

This was first diagnosed in the United States in 1976 in Lyme, CT in people who lived in close proximity to the deer tick. Symptoms may include acute lameness, fever, swelling of joints and loss of appetite. Your veterinarian can advise you if you live in an endemic area.

After your puppy has completed his puppy vaccinations, you will continue to booster the DHLPP once a year. It is customary to booster the rabies one year after the first vaccine and then, depending on where you live, it should be boostered every year or every three years. This depends on your local laws. The Lyme and corona vaccines are boostered annually and it is recommended that the bordetella be boostered every six to eight months.

ANNUAL VISIT

I would like to impress the importance of the annual check up, which would include the booster vaccinations, check for intestinal parasites and test for heartworm. Today in our very busy world it is rush, rush and see "how much you can get for how little." Unbelievably, some non-veterinary businesses have entered into the vaccination business. More harm than good can come to your dog through improper vaccinations, possibly from inferior vaccines and/or the wrong schedule. More than likely you truly care about your companion dog and over the years you have

Your Mini Schnauzer can be subject to parasites like fleas and ticks when outdoors. Be sure to check your dog's coat thoroughly after playing outside.

devoted much time and expense to his well being. Perhaps you are unaware that a vaccination is not just a vaccination. There is more involved. Please, please follow through with regular physical examinations. It is so important for your veterinarian to know your dog and this is especially true during middle age through the geriatric years. More than likely your older dog will require more than one physical a year. The annual physical is good preventive medicine. Through early diagnosis and subsequent treatment your dog can maintain a longer and better quality of life.

INTESTINAL PARASITES

Hookworms

These are almost microscopic intestinal worms that can cause anemia and therefore serious problems, including death, in young puppies. Hookworms can be transmitted to humans through penetration of the skin. Puppies may be born with them.

Roundworms

These are spaghetti-like worms that can cause a potbellied appearance and dull coat along with more severe symptoms, such as vomiting, diarrhea and coughing. Puppies acquire these while in the mother's uterus and through lactation. Both hookworms and roundworms may be acquired through ingestion.

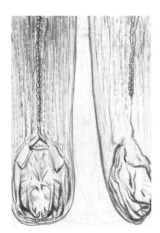

Hookworms are almost microscopic intestinal worms that can cause anemia and therefore serious problems, even death.

Whipworms

These have a three-month life cycle and are not acquired through the dam. They cause intermittent diarrhea usually with mucus. Whipworms are possibly the most difficult worm to eradicate. Their eggs are very resistant to most environmental factors and can last for years until the proper conditions enable them to mature. Whipworms are seldom seen in the stool.

Intestinal parasites are more prevalent in some areas than others. Climate, soil and contamination are big factors contributing to the incidence of intestinal parasites. Eggs are passed in the stool, lay on the ground and then become infective in a certain number of days. Each of the above worms has a different life cycle. Your best chance of becoming and remaining worm-free is to always pooper-scoop your yard. A fenced-in yard keeps stray dogs out, which is certainly helpful. I would recommend having a fecal examination on your dog twice a year or

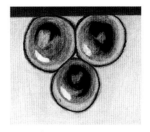

Roundworm eggs, as seen on a fecal evaluation. The eggs must develop for at least 12 days before they are infective.

more often if there is a problem. If your dog has a positive fecal sample, then he will be given the appropriate medication and you will be asked to bring back another stool sample in a certain period of time (depending on the type of worm) and then be rewormed. This process goes on until he has at least two negative samples. The different types of worms require different medications. You will be wasting your money and doing your dog an injustice by buying over-the-counter medication without first consulting your veterinarian.

OTHER INTERNAL PARASITES

Coccidiosis and Giardiasis

These protozoal infections usually affect puppies, especially in places where large numbers of puppies are brought together. Older dogs may harbor these infections but do not show signs unless they are stressed. Symptoms include diarrhea, weight loss and lack of appetite. These infections are not always apparent in the fecal examination.

Tapeworms

Seldom apparent on fecal floatation, they are diagnosed frequently as rice-like segments around the dog's anus and the base of the tail. Tapeworms are long, flat and ribbon like, sometimes several feet in length, and made up of many segments about five-eighths of an inch long. The two most common types of tapeworms found in the dog are:

(1) First the larval form of the flea tapeworm parasite must mature

in an intermediate host, the flea, before it can become infective. Your dog acquires this by ingesting the flea through licking and chewing.

(2) Rabbits, rodents and certain large game animals serve as intermediate hosts for other species of tapeworms. If your dog should eat one of these infected hosts, then he can acquire tapeworms.

HEARTWORM DISEASE

This is a worm that resides in the heart and adjacent blood vessels of the lung that produces microfilaria, which circulate in the bloodstream. It is possible for a dog to be infected with any number of worms from one to a hundred that can be 6 to 14 inches long. It is a life-threatening disease, expensive to treat and easily prevented. Depending on where you live, your veterinarian may recommend a preventive year-round and either an annual or semiannual blood test. The most common preventive is given once a month.

EXTERNAL PARASITES

Fleas

These pests are not only the dog's worst enemy but also enemy to the owner's pocketbook. Preventing is less expensive than treating, but regardless we'd prefer to spend our money elsewhere. Likely, the majority of our dogs are allergic to the bite of a flea, and in many cases it only takes one flea bite. The protein in the flea's saliva is the culprit. Allergic dogs have a reaction, which usually results in a "hot spot." More than likely such a reaction will involve a trip to the veterinarian for treatment. Yes, prevention is less expensive. Fortunately today there are several good products available.

If there is a flea infestation, no one product is going to correct the problem. Not only will the dog require treatment so will the environment. In general flea collars are not very effective although there is now available an "egg" collar that will kill the eggs on the dog. Dips are the most economical but they are messy. There are some effective shampoos and treatments available through pet shops and veterinarians. An oral tablet arrived on the American market in 1995 and was popular in Europe the previous year. It sterilizes the female flea but will not kill adult fleas. Therefore the tablet, which is given monthly, will decrease the flea population but is not a "cure-all." Those dogs that suffer from flea-bite allergy will still be subjected to the bite of the flea. Another popular parasiticide is permethrin, which is applied to the back of the dog in one or two places depending on the dog's weight. This product works as a repellent causing the flea to get "hot feet" and jump off. Do not confuse this product with some of the organophosphates that are also applied to the dog's back.

Some products are not usable on young puppies. Treating fleas should be done under your veterinarian's guidance. Frequently it is necessary to

Bordetella attached to canine cilia. Otherwise known as kennel cough, this highly contagious disease should be vaccinated against routinely.

combine products and the layman does not have the knowledge regarding possible toxicities. It is hard to believe but there are a few dogs that do have a natural resistance to fleas. Nevertheless it would be wise to treat all pets at the same time. Don't forget your cats. Cats just love to prowl the neighborhood and consequently return with unwanted guests.

Adult fleas live on the dog but their eggs drop off the dog into the environment. There they go through four larval stages before reaching adulthood, and thereby are able to jump back on the poor unsuspecting dog. The cycle resumes and takes between 21 to 28 days under ideal conditions. There are environmental products available that will kill both the adult fleas and the larvae.

Ticks

Ticks carry Rocky Mountain Spotted Fever, Lyme disease and can cause tick paralysis. They should be removed with tweezers, trying to pull out the head. The jaws carry disease. There is a tick preventive collar that does an excellent job. The ticks automatically back out on those dogs wearing collars.

Sarcoptic Mange

This is a mite that is difficult to find on skin scrapings. The pinnal reflex is a good indicator of this disease. Rub the ends of the pinna (ear) together and the dog will start scratching with his foot. Sarcoptes are highly contagious to other dogs and to humans although they do not live long on humans. They cause intense itching.

Demodectic Mange

This is a mite that is passed from the dam to her puppies. It affects youngsters age three to ten months. Diagnosis is confirmed by skin scraping. Small areas of alopecia around the eyes, lips and/or forelegs become visible. There is little itching unless there is a secondary bacterial infection. Some breeds are afflicted more than others.

Cheyletiella

This causes intense itching and is diagnosed by skin scraping. It lives in the outer layers of the skin of dogs, cats, rabbits and humans. Yellow-gray scales may be found on the back and the rump, top of the head and the nose.

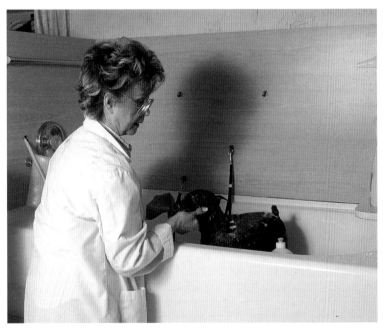

There are a number of shampoos available to help fight off fleas. Check with your veterinarian or local pet shop for recommendations.

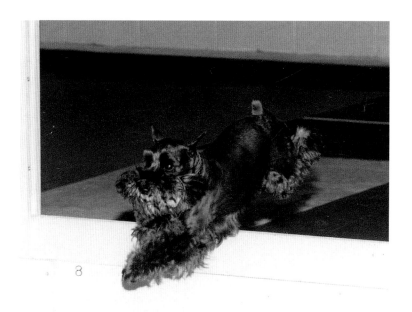

A healthy Miniature Schnauzer can excel in anything he attempts to do. This Mini clears the high jump with ease.

To Breed or Not To Breed

More than likely your breeder has requested that you have your puppy neutered or spayed. Your breeder's request is based on what is healthiest for your dog and what is most beneficial for your breed. Experienced and conscientious breeders devote many years into developing a bloodline. In order to do this, he makes every effort to plan each breeding in regard to conformation, temperament and health. This type of breeder does his best to perform the necessary testing (i.e., OFA, CERF, testing for inherited blood disorders, thyroid, etc.). Testing is expensive and sometimes very disheartening when a favorite dog doesn't pass his health tests. The health history pertains not only to the breeding stock but to the immediate ancestors. Reputable breeders do not want their offspring to be bred indiscriminately. Therefore you may be asked to neuter or spay your puppy. Of course there is always the exception, and your breeder may agree to let you breed your dog under his direct supervision. This is an important concept. More and more effort is being made to breed healthier dogs.

Breeding your dog is a big responsibility and should only be done by people who are experienced and able to offer care to both the mother and any resulting puppies.

Spay/Neuter

There are numerous benefits of performing this surgery at six months of age. Unspayed females are subject to mammary and ovarian cancer. In order to prevent mammary cancer she must be spayed prior to her first heat cycle. Later in life, an unspayed female may develop a pyometra (an infected uterus), which is definitely life threatening.

Spaying is performed under a general anesthetic and is easy on the young dog. As you might expect it is a little harder on the older dog, but that is no reason to deny her the surgery. The surgery removes the ovaries and uterus. It is important to remove all the ovarian tissue. If some is left behind, she could remain attractive to males. In order to view the ovaries, a reasonably long incision is necessary. An ovariohysterectomy is considered major surgery.

Neutering the male at a young age will inhibit some characteristic male behavior that owners frown upon. Some boys will not hike their legs and mark territory if they are neutered at six months of age. Also neutering at a young age has hormonal benefits, lessening the chance of hormonal aggressiveness.

Surgery involves removing the testicles but leaving the scrotum. If there should be a retained testicle, then he definitely needs to be neutered before the age of two or three years. Retained testicles can develop into cancer. Unneutered males are at risk for testicular cancer, perineal fistulas, perianal tumors and fistulas and prostatic disease.

Intact males and females are prone to housebreaking accidents. Females urinate frequently before, during and after heat cycles, and males tend to mark territory if there is a female in heat. Males may show the same behavior if there is a visiting dog or guests.

Surgery involves a sterile operating procedure equivalent to human surgery. The incision site is shaved, surgically scrubbed and draped. The veterinarian wears a sterile surgical gown, cap, mask and gloves. Anesthesia should be monitored by a registered technician. It is customary for the veterinarian to recommend a pre-anesthetic blood screening, looking for metabolic problems and a ECG rhythm strip to check for normal heart function. Today anesthetics are equal to human anesthetics, which enables your dog to walk out of the clinic the same day as surgery.

Some folks worry about their dog gaining weight after being neutered or spayed. This is usually not the case. It is true that some dogs may be less active so they could develop a problem, but most dogs are just as active as they were before surgery. However, if your dog should begin to gain, then you need to decrease his food and see to it that he gets a little more exercise.

DENTAL CARE for Your Dog's Life

S o you've got a new puppy! You also have a new set of puppy teeth in your household. Anyone who has ever raised a puppy is abundantly aware of these new teeth. Your puppy will chew anything it can reach, chase your shoelaces, and play "tear the rag" with any piece of clothing it can find. When puppies are newly born, they have no teeth. At about four weeks of age, puppies of most breeds begin to develop their deciduous or baby teeth. They begin eating semi-solid food, fighting and biting with their litter mates, and learning discipline from their mother. As their new teeth come in, they inflict more pain on their mother's breasts, so her feeding sessions become less frequent and shorter. By six or eight weeks, the mother will start growling to warn her pups when they are fighting too roughly or hurting her as they nurse too much with their new teeth.

Puppies need to chew. It is a necessary part of their physical and mental development. They develop muscles and necessary life skills as they drag objects around, fight over possession, and vocalize alerts and warnings. Puppies chew on things to explore their world. They are using their sense of taste to determine what is food and

Good oral hygiene is important to your Miniature Schnauzer's overall health and well-being.

A thorough oral examination should be a part of your Mini Schnauzer's regular checkup.

what is not. How else can they tell an electrical cord from a lizard? At about four months of age, most puppies begin shedding their baby teeth. Often these teeth need some help to come out and make way for the permanent teeth. The incisors (front teeth) will be replaced first. Then, the adult canine or fang teeth erupt. When the baby tooth is not shed before the permanent tooth comes in, veterinarians call it a retained deciduous tooth. This condition will often cause gum infections by trapping hair and debris between the permanent tooth and the retained baby tooth. Nylafloss® is an excellent device for puppies to use. They can toss it, drag it, and chew on the many surfaces it presents. The baby teeth can catch in the nylon material, aiding in their removal. Puppies that have adequate chew toys will have less destructive behavior, develop more physically, and have less chance of retained deciduous teeth.

During the first year, your dog should be seen by your veterinarian at regular intervals. Your veterinarian will let you know when to bring in your puppy for vaccinations and parasite examinations. At each visit, your veterinarian should inspect the lips, teeth, and mouth as part of a complete physical examination. You should take some part in the maintenance of your dog's oral health. You should examine your dog's mouth weekly throughout his first year to make sure there are no sores, foreign objects, tooth problems, etc. If your dog drools excessively, shakes its head, or has bad breath, consult

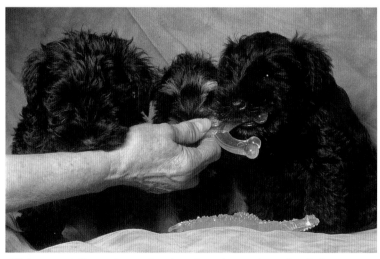

All dogs, especially puppies, need to chew. Provide your dog with safe chew toys.

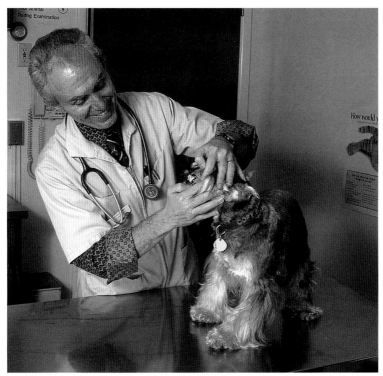

During your annual checkup at the vet, have him exam your dog's teeth for excessive plaque buildup. If necessary, he can clean the teeth at this time.

your veterinarian. By the time your dog is six months old, the permanent teeth are all in and plaque can start to accumulate on the tooth surfaces. This is when your dog needs to develop good dental-care habits to prevent calculus build-up on its teeth. Brushing is best. That is a fact that cannot be denied. However, some dogs do not like their teeth brushed regularly, or you may not be able to accomplish the task. In that case, you should consider a product that will help prevent plaque and calculus build-up.

The Dental Chews® and Galileo Bone® are other excellent choices for the first three years of a dog's life. Their shapes make them interesting for the dog. As the dog chews on them, the solid polyurethane massages the gums which improves the blood circulation to the periodontal tissues. Projections on the chew devices increase the surface and are in contact with the tooth for more efficient cleaning. The unique shape and consistency prevent your dog from exerting excessive force on his own teeth or from breaking off pieces of the bone. If your dog is an aggressive chewer or weighs more than 55 pounds (25 kg), you should consider giving him a Nylabone®, the most durable chew product on the market.

The Gumabones®, made by the Nylabone Company, is constructed of strong polyurethane, which is softer than nylon. Less powerful chewers prefer the Gumabones® to the Nylabones®. A super option for your dog is the Hercules Bone®, a uniquely shaped bone named after the great Olympian for its exception strength. Like all Nylabone products, they are specially scented to make them attractive to your dog. Ask your veterinarian about these bones and he will validate the good doctor's prescription: Nylabones® not only give your dog a good chewing workout but also help to save your dog's teeth (and even his life, as it protects him from possible fatal periodontal diseases).

By the time dogs are four years old, 75% of them have periodontal disease. It is the most common infection in dogs. Yearly examinations by your veterinarian are essential to maintaining your dog's good health. If your veterinarian detects periodontal disease, he or she may recommend a prophylactic cleaning. To do a thorough cleaning, it will be necessary to put your dog under anesthesia. With modern gas anesthetics and monitoring equipment, the procedure is pretty safe. Your veterinarian will scale the teeth with an ultrasound scaler or hand instrument. This removes the calculus from the teeth. If there are calculus deposits below the gum line, the veterinarian will plane the roots to make them smooth. After all of the calculus has been removed, the teeth are polished with pumice in a polishing cup. If any medical or surgical treatment is needed, it is done at this time. The final step would be fluoride treatment and your follow-up treatment at home. If the periodontal disease is advanced, the veterinarian may prescribe a medicated mouth rinse or antibiotics for use at home. Make sure your dog has safe, clean and attractive chew toys and treats. Chooz® treats are another way of using a consumable treat to help keep your dog's teeth clean.

Rawhide is the most popular of all materials for a dog to chew. This has never been good news to dog owners, because rawhide is inherently very dangerous for dogs. Thousands of dogs have died from rawhide, having swallowed the hide after it has become soft and mushy, only to cause stomach and intestinal blockage. A new rawhide product on the market has finally solved the problem of

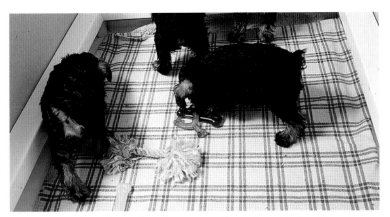

Make sure you have plenty of toys for your puppies to play with. It will exercise their teeth and gums and keep them out of trouble.

rawhide: molded Roar-Hide® from Nylabone. These are composed of processed, cut up, and melted American rawhide injected into your dog's favorite shape: a dog bone. These dog-safe devices smell and taste like rawhide but don't break up. The ridges on the bones help to fight tartar build-up on the teeth and they last ten times longer than the usual rawhide chews.

As your dog ages, professional examination and cleaning should become more frequent. The mouth should be inspected at least once a year. Your veterinarian may recommend visits every six months. In the geriatric patient, organs such as the heart, liver, and kidneys do not function as well as when they were young. Your veterinarian will probably want to test these organs' functions prior to using general anesthesia for dental cleaning. If your dog is a good chewer and you work closely with your veterinarian, your dog can keep all of its teeth all of its life. However, as your dog ages, his sense of smell, sight, and taste will diminish. He may not have the desire to chase, trap or chew his toys. He will also not have the energy to chew for long periods, as arthritis and periodontal disease make chewing painful. This will leave you with more responsibility for keeping his teeth clean and healthy. The dog that would not let you brush his teeth at one year of age, may let you brush his teeth now that he is ten years old.

If you train your dog with good chewing habits as a puppy, he will have healthier teeth throughout his life.

135

IDENTIFICATION and Finding the Lost Dog

There are several ways of identifying your dog. The old standby is a collar with dog license, rabies, and ID tags. Unfortunately collars have a way of being separated from the dog and tags fall off. We're not suggesting you shouldn't use a collar and tags. If they stay intact and on the dog, they are the quickest way of identification.

For several years owners have been tattooing their dogs. Some tattoos use a number with a registry. Here lies the problem because there are several registries to check. If you wish to tattoo, use your social security number. The humane shelters have the means to trace it. It is usually done on the inside of the rear thigh. The area is first shaved and numbed. There is no pain, although a few dogs do not like the buzzing sound. Occasionally tattooing is not legible and needs to be redone.

The newest method of identification is microchipping. The microchip is a computer chip that is no larger than a grain of rice.

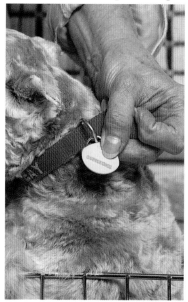

Your Miniature Schnauzer should wear a collar and identification tags at all times in case he becomes separated from you.

The veterinarian implants it by injection between the shoulder blades. The dog feels no discomfort. If your dog is lost and picked up by the humane society, they can trace you by scanning the microchip, which has its own code. Microchip scanners are friendly to other brands of microchips and their registries. The microchip comes with a dog tag saying the dog is microchipped. It is the safest way of identifying your dog.

FINDING THE LOST DOG

I am sure you will agree that there would be little worse than losing your dog. Responsible pet owners rarely lose their dogs.

They do not let their dogs run free because they don't want harm to come to them. Not only that but in most, if not all, states there is a leash law.

Beware of fenced-in yards. They can be a hazard. Dogs find ways to escape either over or under the fence. Another fast exit is through the gate that perhaps the neighbor's child left unlocked.

Below is a list that hopefully will be of help to you if you need it. Remember don't give up, keep looking. Your dog is worth your efforts.

1. Contact your neighbors and put flyers with a photo on it in their mailboxes. Information you should include would be the dog's name, breed, sex, color, age, source of identification, when your dog was last seen and where, and your name and phone numbers. It may be helpful to say the dog needs medical care. Offer a *reward*.

2. Check all local shelters daily. It is also possible for your dog to be picked up away from home and end up in an out-of-the-way shelter. Check these too. Go in person. It is not good enough to call. Most shelters are limited on the time they can hold dogs then they are put up for adoption or euthanized. There is the possibility that your dog will not make it to the shelter for several days. Your dog could have been wandering or someone may have tried to keep him.

3. Notify all local veterinarians. Call and send flyers.

4. Call your breeder. Frequently breeders are contacted when one of their breed is found.

5. Contact the rescue group for your breed.

6. Contact local schools—children may have seen your dog.

7. Post flyers at the schools, groceries, gas stations, convenience stores, veterinary clinics, groomers and any other place that will allow them.

8. Advertise in the newspaper.

9. Advertise on the radio.

TRAVELING with Your Dog

The earlier you start traveling with your new puppy or dog, the better. He needs to become accustomed to traveling. However, some dogs are nervous riders and become carsick easily. It is helpful if he starts with an empty stomach. Do not despair, as it will go better if you continue taking him with you on short fun rides. How would you feel if every time you rode in the car you stopped at the doctor's for an injection? You would soon dread that nasty car. Older dogs that tend to get carsick may have more of a problem adjusting to traveling. Those dogs that are having a serious problem may benefit from some medication prescribed by the veterinarian.

Do give your dog a chance to relieve himself before getting into the car. It is a good idea to be prepared for a clean up with a leash, paper towels, bag and terry cloth towel.

The safest place for your dog is in a fiberglass crate, although close confinement can promote carsickness in some dogs. If your dog is nervous you can try letting him ride on the seat next to you or in someone's lap.

An alternative to the crate would be to use a car harness made for dogs and/or a safety strap attached to the harness or collar. Whatever you do, do not let your dog ride in the back of a pickup truck unless he is securely tied on a very short lead. I've seen trucks stop quickly and, even though the dog was tied, it fell out and was dragged.

Because of his easygoing nature, the Mini Schnauzer can adapt to almost any environment.

Your Miniature Schnauzer loves to travel with you. Take him with you as often as possible.

Another advantage of the crate is that it is a safe place to leave him if you need to run into the store. Otherwise you wouldn't be able to leave the windows down. Keep in mind that while many dogs are overly protective in their crates, this may not be enough to deter dognappers. In some states it is against the law to leave a dog in the car unattended.

Never leave a dog loose in the car wearing a collar and leash. More than one dog has killed himself by hanging. Do not let him put his head out an open window. Foreign debris can be blown into his eyes. When leaving your dog unattended in a car, consider the temperature. It can take less than five minutes to reach temperatures over 100 degrees Fahrenheit.

TRIPS

Perhaps you are taking a trip. Give consideration to what is best for your dog—traveling with you or boarding. When traveling by car, van or motor home, you need to think ahead about locking your vehicle. In all probability you have many valuables in the car and do not wish to leave it unlocked. Perhaps most valuable and not replaceable is your dog. Give thought to

Given the proper care, your Miniature Schnauzer will be a lifelong companion.

Even on vacation, the Mini Schnauzer will look for a task to keep him busy. Maxwell and Black Jack help friends water the flowers.

securing your vehicle and providing adequate ventilation for him. Another consideration for you when traveling with your dog is medical problems that may arise and little inconveniences, such as exposure to external parasites. Some areas of the country are quite flea infested. You may want to carry flea spray with you. This is even a good idea when staying in motels. Quite possibly you are not the only occupant of the room.

Unbelievably many motels and even hotels do allow canine guests, even some very first-class ones. Gaines Pet Foods Corporation publishes *Touring With Towser*, a directory of domestic hotels and motels that accommodate guests with dogs. Their address is Gaines TWT, PO Box 5700, Kankakee, IL, 60902. Call ahead to any motel that you may be considering and see if they accept pets. Sometimes it is necessary to pay a deposit against room damage. The management may feel reassured if you mention that your dog will be crated. If you do travel with your dog, take along plenty of baggies so that you can clean up after him. When we all do our share in cleaning up, we make it possible for motels to continue accepting our pets. As a matter of fact, you should practice cleaning up everywhere you take your dog.

Depending on where your are traveling, you may need an up-to-date health certificate issued by your veterinarian. It is good policy to take along your dog's medical information, which would include the name, address and phone number of your veterinarian, vaccination record, rabies certificate, and any medication he is taking.

AIR TRAVEL

When traveling by air, you need to contact the airlines to check their policy. Usually you have to make arrangements up to a couple of weeks in advance for traveling with your dog. The airlines require your dog to travel in an airline approved fiberglass crate. Usually these can be purchased through the airlines but they are also readily available in most pet-supply stores. If your dog is not accustomed to a crate, then it is a good idea to get him acclimated to it before your trip. The day of the actual trip you should withhold water about one hour ahead of departure and no food for about 12 hours. The airlines generally have temperature restrictions, which do not allow pets to travel if it is either too cold or too hot. Frequently these restrictions are based on the temperatures at the departure and arrival airports. It's best to inquire about a health certificate. These usually need to be issued within ten days of departure. You should arrange for non-stop, direct flights and if a commuter plane should be involved, check to see if it will carry dogs. Some don't. The Humane Society of the United States has put together a tip sheet for airline traveling. You can receive a copy by sending a self-addressed stamped envelope to:

The Humane Society of the United States
Tip Sheet
2100 L Street NW
Washington, DC 20037.

Regulations differ for traveling outside of the country and are sometimes changed without notice. Well in advance you need to write or call the appropriate consulate or agricultural department for instructions. Some countries have lengthy quarantines (six months), and countries differ in their rabies vaccination requirements. For instance, it may have to be given at least 30 days ahead of your departure.

Do make sure your dog is wearing proper identification including your name, phone number and city. You never know when you might be in an accident and separated from your dog. Or your dog could be frightened and somehow manage to escape and run away.

Another suggestion would be to carry in-case-of-emergency instructions. These would include the address and phone number of a relative or friend, your veterinarian's name, address and phone number, and your dog's medical information.

If your Mini Schnauzer accompanies you on vacation, make sure to bring his blanket and toys to make him more comfortable.

Boarding Kennels

Perhaps you have decided that you need to board your dog. Your veterinarian can recommend a good boarding facility or possibly a pet sitter that will come to your house. It is customary for the boarding kennel to ask for proof of vaccination for the DHLPP, rabies and bordetella vaccine. The bordetella should have been given within six months of boarding. This is for your protection. If they do not ask for this proof I would not board at their kennel. Ask about flea control. Those dogs that suffer flea-bite allergy can get in trouble at a boarding kennel. Unfortunately boarding kennels are limited on how much they are able to do.

For more information on pet sitting, contact NAPPS:
National Association of Professional Pet Sitters
1200 G Street, NW
Suite 760
Washington, DC 20005.

Some pet clinics have technicians that pet sit and technicians that board clinic patients in their homes. This may be an alternative for you. Ask your veterinarian if they have an employee that can help you. There is a definite advantage of having a technician care for your dog, especially if your dog is on medication or is a senior citizen.

You can write for a copy of *Traveling With Your Pet* from ASPCA, Education Department, 441 E. 92nd Street, New York, NY 10128.

BEHAVIOR and Canine Communication

Studies of the human/animal bond point out the importance of the unique relationships that exist between people and their pets. Those of us who share our lives with pets understand the special part they play through companionship, service and protection. For many, the pet/owner bond goes beyond simple companionship; pets are often considered members of the family. A leading pet food manufacturer recently conducted a nationwide survey of pet owners to gauge just how important pets were in their lives. Here's what they found:
- 76 percent allow their pets to sleep on their beds
- 78 percent think of their pets as their children
- 84 percent display photos of their pets, mostly in their homes
- 84 percent think that their pets react to their own emotions
- 100 percent talk to their pets
- 97 percent think that their pets understand what they're saying
  Are you surprised?

Senior citizens show more concern for their own eating habits when they have the responsibility of feeding a dog. Seeing that their dog is routinely exercised encourages the owner to think of schedules that otherwise may seem unimportant to the senior citizen. The older owner may be arthritic and feeling poorly but with responsibility for his dog he has a reason to get up and get moving. It is a big plus if his dog is an attention seeker who will demand such from his owner.

Over the last couple of decades, it has been shown that pets relieve the stress of those who lead busy lives. Owning a pet has been known to lessen the occurrence of heart attack and stroke.

Many single folks thrive on the companionship of a dog. Lifestyles are very different from a long time ago, and today more individuals seek the single life. However, they receive fulfillment from owning a dog.

Most likely the majority of our dogs live in family environments. The companionship they provide is well worth the effort involved. In my opinion, every child should have the opportunity to have a family dog. Dogs teach responsibility through understanding their care, feelings and even respecting their life cycles. Frequently those children who have not been exposed to dogs grow up afraid of dogs,

The bond between owner and dog is a strong one. Who could help but smile at these adorable puppies?

which isn't good. Dogs sense timidity and some will take advantage of the situation.

Today more dogs are serving as service dogs. Since the origination of the Seeing Eye dogs years ago, we now have trained hearing dogs. Also dogs are trained to provide service for the handicapped and are able to perform many different tasks for their owners. Search and Rescue dogs, with their handlers, are sent throughout the world to assist in recovery of disaster victims. They are life savers.

Therapy dogs are very popular with nursing homes, and some hospitals even allow them to visit. The inhabitants truly look forward to their visits. They wanted and were allowed to have visiting dogs in their beds to hold and love.

Nationally there is a Pet Awareness Week to educate students and others about the value and basic care of our pets. Many countries take an even greater interest in their pets than Americans do. In those countries the pets are allowed to accompany their owners into restaurants and shops, etc. In the U.S. this freedom is only available to our service dogs. Even so we think very highly of the human/animal bond.

CANINE BEHAVIOR

Canine behavior problems are the number-one reason for pet owners to dispose of their dogs, either through new homes, humane shelters or euthanasia. Unfortunately there are too many owners who are unwilling to devote the necessary time to properly train their dogs. On the other hand, there are those who not only are concerned about inherited health problems but are also aware of the dog's mental stability.

You may realize that a breed and his group relatives (i.e., sporting, hounds, etc.) show tendencies to behavioral characteristics. An experienced breeder can acquaint you with his breed's personality. Unfortunately many breeds are labeled with poor temperaments when actually the breed as a whole is not affected but only a small percentage of individuals within the breed.

Inheritance and environment contribute to the dog's behavior. Some naïve people suggest inbreeding as the cause of bad temperaments. Inbreeding only results in poor behavior if the ancestors carry the trait. If there are excellent temperaments behind the dogs, then inbreeding will promote good temperaments in the offspring. Did you ever consider that inbreeding is what sets the characteristics of a breed? A purebred dog is the end result of inbreeding. This does not spare the mixed-breed dog from the same problems. Mixed-breed dogs frequently are the offspring of purebred dogs.

Not too many decades ago most of our dogs led a different lifestyle than what is prevalent today. Usually mom stayed home so the dog had human companionship and someone to discipline it if needed. Not much was expected from the dog. Today's mom works and everyone's life is at a much faster pace.

The dog may have to adjust to being a "weekend" dog. The family is gone all day during the week, and the dog is left to his own devices for entertainment. Some dogs sleep all day waiting for their family to come home and others become wigwam wreckers if given the opportunity. Crates do ensure the safety of the dog and the house. However, he could become a physically and emotionally cripple if he doesn't get enough exercise and attention. We still appreciate and want the companionship of our dogs although we expect more from them. In many cases we tend to forget dogs are just that—*dogs* not human beings.

Taking responsibility for a dog can give a person a purpose in life. Of course, playing with a Mini Schnauzer can brighten anyone's day.

SOCIALIZING AND TRAINING

Many prospective puppy buyers lack experience regarding the proper socialization and training needed to develop the type of pet we all desire. In the first 18 months, training does take some work. It is easier to start proper training before there is a problem that needs to be corrected.

The initial work begins with the breeder. The breeder should start socializing the puppy at five to six weeks of age and cannot let up. Human socializing is critical up through 12 weeks of age and likewise important during the following months. The litter should be left together during the first few weeks but it is necessary to separate them by ten weeks of age. Leaving them together after that time will increase competition for litter dominance. If puppies are not socialized with people by 12 weeks of age, they will be timid in later life.

The eight- to ten-week age period is a fearful time for puppies. They need to be handled very gently around children and adults. There should be no harsh discipline during this time. Starting at 14 weeks of age, the puppy begins the juvenile period, which ends when he reaches sexual maturity around six to 14 months of age. During the juvenile period he needs to be introduced to strangers (adults, children

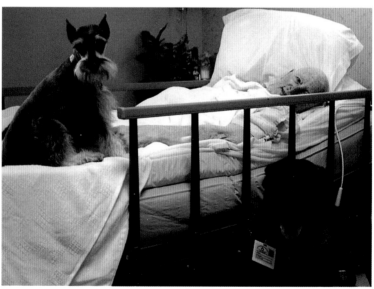

It has been proven that spending time with a dog can reduce stress and improve the quality of your life. Maxwell and Kipper visit a nursing home patient.

Early socialization with other pets will help your Mini Schnauzer later in life. This Mini tries to get a new acquaintance to come out of his shell and make friends.

and other dogs) on the home property. At sexual maturity he will begin to bark at strangers and become more protective. Males start to lift their legs to urinate but if you desire you can inhibit this behavior by walking your boy on leash away from trees, shrubs, fences, etc.

Perhaps you are thinking about an older puppy. You need to inquire about the puppy's social experience. If he has lived in a kennel, he may have a hard time adjusting to people and environmental stimuli. Assuming he has had a good social upbringing, there are advantages to an older puppy.

Training includes puppy kindergarten and a minimum of one to two basic training classes. During these classes you will learn how to dominate your youngster. This is especially important if you own a large breed of dog. It is somewhat harder, if not nearly impossible, for some owners to be the Alpha figure when their dog towers over them. You will be taught how to properly restrain your dog. This concept is important. Again it puts you in the Alpha position. All dogs need to be restrained many times during their lives. Believe it or not, some of our worst offenders are the eight-week-old puppies that are brought to our clinic. They need to be gently restrained for a nail trim but the way they carry on you would think we were killing them. In comparison, their vaccination is a "piece of cake." When we ask dogs to do something that is not agreeable to them, then their worst comes out. Life will be easier for your dog if you expose him at a young age to the necessities of life—proper behavior and restraint.

Understanding the Dog's Language

Most authorities agree that the dog is a descendent of the wolf. The dog and wolf have similar traits. For instance both are pack oriented and prefer not to be isolated for long periods of time. Another characteristic is that the dog, like the wolf, looks to the leader—Alpha—for direction. Both the wolf and the dog communicate through body language, not only within their pack but with outsiders.

Every pack has an Alpha figure. The dog looks to you, or should look to you, to be that leader. If your dog doesn't receive the proper training and guidance, he very well may replace you as Alpha. This would be a serious problem and is certainly a disservice to your dog.

Eye contact is one way the Alpha wolf keeps order within his pack. You are Alpha so you must establish eye contact with your puppy. Obviously your puppy will have to look at you. Practice eye contact even if you need to hold his head for five to ten seconds at a time. You can give him a treat as a reward. Make sure your eye contact is gentle and not threatening. Later, if he has been naughty, it is permissible to give him a long, penetrating look. There are some older dogs that never learned eye contact as puppies and cannot accept eye contact. You should avoid eye contact with these dogs since they feel threatened and will retaliate as such.

Well-socialized Miniature Schnauzers get along with anybody! Black Jack and Maxwell pose for a picture with their buddy Alana, a Portuguese Water Dog.

Most Miniature Schnauzers are treated like members of the family, and as such, need to conform to household rules.

BODY LANGUAGE

The play bow, when the forequarters are down and the hindquarters are elevated, is an invitation to play. Puppies play fight, which helps them learn the acceptable limits of biting. This is necessary for later in their lives. Nevertheless, an owner may be falsely reassured by the playful nature of his dog's aggression. Playful aggression toward another dog or human may be an indication of serious aggression in the future. Owners should never play fight or play tug-of-war with any dog that is inclined to be dominant.

Signs of submission are:
1. Avoids eye contact.
2. Active submission—the dog crouches down, ears back and the tail is lowered.
3. Passive submission—the dog rolls on his side with his hindlegs in the air and frequently urinates.

Signs of dominance are:

Puppy kindergarten will help your young Miniature Schnauzer become a well-mannered companion.

    1. Makes eye contact.

    2. Stands with ears up, tail up and the hair raised on his neck.

    3. Shows dominance over another dog by standing at right angles over it.

Dominant dogs tend to behave in characteristic ways such as:

    1. The dog may be unwilling to move from his place (i.e., reluctant to give up the sofa if the owner wants to sit there).

    2. He may not part with toys or objects in his mouth and may show possessiveness with his food bowl.

    3. He may not respond quickly to commands.

    4. He may be disagreeable for grooming and dislikes to be petted.

Dogs are popular because of their sociable nature. Those that have contact with humans during the first 12 weeks of life regard them as a member of their own species—their pack. All dogs have the potential for both dominant and submissive behavior. Only through experience and training do they learn to whom it is appropriate to show which behavior. Not all dogs are concerned with dominance but owners need to be aware of that potential. It is wise for the owner to establish his dominance early on.

A human can express dominance or submission toward a dog in the following ways:

1. Meeting the dog's gaze signals dominance. Averting the gaze signals submission. If the dog growls or threatens, averting the gaze is the first avoiding action to take—it may prevent attack. It is important to establish eye contact in the puppy. The older dog that has not been exposed to eye contact may see it as a threat and will not be willing to submit.

2. Being taller than the dog signals dominance; being lower signals submission. This is why, when attempting to make friends with a strange dog or catch the runaway, one should kneel down to his level. Some owners see their dogs become dominant when allowed on the furniture or on the bed. Then he is at the owner's level.

3. An owner can gain dominance by ignoring all the dog's social initiatives. The owner pays attention to the dog only when he obeys a command.

No dog should be allowed to achieve dominant status over any adult or child. Ways of preventing are as follows:

Body language is one way to tell what your dog is feeling. These two Miniature Schnauzers look like they just want to have fun!

1. Handle the puppy gently, especially during the three- to four-month period.
2. Let the children and adults handfeed him and teach him to take food without lunging or grabbing.
3. Do not allow him to chase children or joggers.
4. Do not allow him to jump on people or mount their legs. Even females may be inclined to mount. It is not only a male habit.
5. Do not allow him to growl for any reason.
6. Don't participate in wrestling or tug-of-war games.
7. Don't physically punish puppies for aggressive behavior. Restrain him from repeating the infraction and teach an alternative behavior. Dogs should earn everything they receive from their owners. This would include sitting to receive petting or treats, sitting before going out the door and sitting to receive the collar and leash. These types of exercises reinforce the owner's dominance.

Young children should never be left alone with a dog. It i' important that children learn some basic obedience commands sc they have some control over the dog. They will gain the respect of their dog.

FEAR

One of the most common problems dogs experience is being fearful. Some dogs are more afraid than others. On the lesser side, which is sometimes humorous to watch, dogs can be afraid of a strange object. They act silly when something is out of place in the house. We call his problem perceptive intelligence. He realizes the abnormal within his known environment. He does not react the same way in strange environments since he does not know what is normal.

On the more serious side is a fear of people. This can result in backing off, seeking his own space and saying "leave me alone" or it can result in an aggressive behavior that may lead to challenging the person. Respect that the dog wants to be left alone and give him time to come forward. If you approach the cornered dog, he may resort to snapping. If you leave him alone, he may decide to come forward, which should be rewarded with a treat.

Some dogs may initially be too fearful to take treats. In these cases it is helpful to make sure the dog hasn't eaten for about 24 hours.

Being a little hungry encourages him to accept the treats, especially if they are of the "gourmet" variety.

Dogs can be afraid of numerous things, including loud noises and thunderstorms. Invariably the owner rewards (by comforting) the dog when it shows signs of fearfulness. When your dog is frightened, direct his attention to something else and act happy. Don't dwell on his fright.

AGGRESSION

Some different types of aggression are: predatory, defensive, dominance, possessive, protective, fear induced, noise provoked, "rage" syndrome (unprovoked aggression), maternal and aggression directed toward other dogs. Aggression is the most common behavioral problem encountered. Protective breeds are expected to be more aggressive than others but with the proper upbringing they can make very dependable companions. You need to be able to read your dog.

Some young dogs may be fearful of certain things. Be patient and let your Mini Schnauzer become used to the situation.

Many factors contribute to aggression including genetics and environment. An improper environment, which may include the living conditions, lack of social life, excessive punishment, being attacked or frightened by an aggressive dog, etc., can all influence a dog's behavior. Even spoiling him and giving too much praise may be detrimental. Isolation and the lack of human contact or exposure to frequent teasing by children or adults also can ruin a good dog.

Lack of direction, fear, or confusion lead to aggression in those dogs that are so inclined. Any obedience exercise, even the sit and down, can direct the dog and overcome fear and/or confusion. Every dog should learn these commands as a youngster, and there should be periodic reinforcement.

When a dog is showing signs of aggression, you should speak calmly (no screaming or hysterics) and firmly give a command that he understands, such as the sit. As soon as your dog obeys, you have assumed your dominant position. Aggression presents

Your Mini Schnauzer can use his training in all types of situations. Bee's BB Gunn uses his sit for a Fourth of July photo.

Never underestimate your Miniature Schnauzer's ability to get into mischief! Your puppy should be properly supervised at all times.

a problem because there may be danger to others. Sometimes it is an emotional issue. Owners may consciously or unconsciously encourage their dog's aggression. Other owners show responsibility by accepting the problem and taking measures to keep it under control. The owner is responsible for his dog's actions, and it is not wise to take a chance on someone being bitten, especially a child. Euthanasia is the solution for some owners and in severe cases this may be the best choice. However, few dogs are that dangerous and very few are that much of a threat to their owners. If caution is exercised and professional help is gained early on, most cases can be controlled.

Some authorities recommend feeding a lower protein (less than 20 percent) diet. They believe this can aid in reducing aggression. If the dog loses weight, then vegetable oil can be added. Veterinarians and behaviorists are having some success

The Miniature Schnauzer is an intelligent dog, and with the proper socialization and training, can become the perfect companion.

with pharmacology. In many cases treatment is possible and can improve the situation.

If you have done everything according to "the book" regarding training and socializing and are still having a behavior problem, don't procrastinate. It is important that the problem gets attention before it is out of hand. It is estimated that 20 percent of a veterinarian's time may be devoted to dealing with problems before they become so intolerable that the dog is separated from its home and owner. If your veterinarian isn't able to help, he should refer you to a behaviorist.

RESOURCES

American Miniature Schnauzer Club, Inc.
Corresponding Secretary: Terrie Houck
209 Pine Road
Mt Holly, NC 28120-9650
http://www.amsc.us

American Kennel Club
Headquarters:
260 Madison Avenue
New York, NY 10016

Operations Center:
5580 Centerview Drive
Raleigh, NC 27606-3390

Customer Services:
Phone: (919) 233-9767
Fax: (919) 816-3627
http://www.akc.org

The Kennel Club
1 Clarges Street
Picadilly, London WIY 8AB, England
http://www.the-kennel-club-org.uk

The Canadian Kennel Club
89 Skyway Avenue
Suite 100
Etobicoke, Ontario,
Canada M9W 6R4
http://www.ckc.ca

The United Kennel Club, Inc.
100 E. Kilgore Road
Kalamazoo, MI 49002-5584
(616) 343-9020
http://www.ukcdogs.com

INDEX